Genteel Rhetoric

Studies in Rhetoric/Communication
Thomas W. Benson, Series Editor

Genteel Rhetoric

Writing High Culture in Nineteenth-Century Boston

Dorothy C. Broaddus

UNIVERSITY OF SOUTH CAROLINA PRESS

© 1999 University of South Carolina

Published in Columbia, South Carolina, by the
University of South Carolina Press

Manufactured in the United States of America

03 02 01 00 99   5 4 3 2 1

Library of Congress Cataloging-in-Publication Data

Broaddus, Dorothy C.
    Genteel rhetoric : writing high culture in nineteenth-century Boston /
Dorothy C. Broaddus.
        p.   cm. — (Studies in rhetoric/communication)
    Includes bibliographical references (p.   ) and index.

    ISBN 1-57003-244-0
    1. American literature—Massachusetts—Boston—History and criticism.
    2. Rhetoric—Social aspects—Massachusetts—Boston—History—19th century.
    3. English language—Rhetoric—Study and teaching—Massachusetts—Boston.
    4. Language and culture—Massachusetts—Boston—History—19th century.
    5. Unitarians—Massachusetts—Boston—Intellectual life.   6. Boston (Mass.)—
    Intellectual life—19th century.   7. Higginson, Thomas Wentworth, 1823–1911
    —Technique.   8. Holmes, Oliver Wendell, 1809–1894—Technique.   9. Lowell,
    James Russell, 1819–1891—Technique.   10. Emerson, Ralph Waldo, 1803–1882
    —Technique.   I. Title.   II. Series.
    PS255.B6 B76   1999
    810.9'974461—ddc21

                                                                    98-19678

This book is for those who can use it—the infiltrators

Contents

Series Editor's Preface

The University of South Carolina Press Studies in Rhetoric/Communication was founded under the editorship of the late Carroll C. Arnold, then professor emeritus at the Pennsylvania State University. Following Arnold's original vision, the series seeks to publish the best contemporary scholarship in the broadly interdisciplinary realms of rhetoric and communication.

In *Genteel Rhetoric,* Dorothy Broaddus examines the rhetoric of high culture in nineteenth-century Boston. Broaddus concentrates on Ralph Waldo Emerson, James Russell Lowell, Oliver Wendell Holmes, and Thomas Wentworth Higginson, all in or influenced by the Unitarian tradition. Though situating these men firmly in their own time and place and interpreting them with admiration, Broaddus also appeals to a larger historical, political, and theoretical frame to resist what she identifies as their condescension and their appeal to universal moral absolutes, leading to the petrification of an impulse of enlightenment and transcendence into a rhetoric of reaction.

All four of these men trained at Harvard, where they studied rhetoric with Edward T. Channing, the Boylston Professor of Rhetoric and Oratory. Channing taught a rhetoric of taste, reason, and character, cultivated through study, practice, and imitation. It was only natural, he taught, that the cultivated and literate should instruct and dominate the society of ordinary people.

Broaddus reads Emerson as a self-invented author who wrote and spoke unconventional sentiments in support of the conventions of elite New England high culture. Lowell, Broaddus argues, celebrated an American democracy properly guided by universal moral absolutes and led by the cultural elite. Holmes celebrated the achievement of a coherent, virtuous, unified self best expressed in the natural aristocracy of the Boston elite. Higginson, an abolitionist and reformer, was Emily Dickinson's editor, urging upon her the standards of his own version of genteel rhetoric.

Broaddus guides us through the rhetoric of these four authors as young men in the New England Renaissance and as mature writers struggling against new contradictions and social forces of the Civil War era, after which their rhetoric came to seem irrelevant or academic, and its appeal to universal moral coherence came to seem mythical, constructed, and artificial. Students of rhetoric will find in Professor Broaddus's book a challenging dialogue with American history and culture; a scrupulous re-reading of Emerson, Lowell, Holmes, and Higginson; and a bracing reconsideration of assumptions about race, class, and gender in the rhetoric of reform.

Thomas W. Benson

Preface

In 1838, William Ellery Channing, famous Boston Unitarian minister, took the lessons of his brother, Harvard's rhetoric professor Edward Tyrell Channing, to the masses when he lectured to the Mechanic Apprentices' Library Association on "Self-Culture." He told the white working-class men the following: "The principle distinction between what are called gentlemen and the vulgar lies in this, that the latter are awkward in manners, and are especially wanting in propriety, clearness, grace, and force of utterance. A man who cannot open his lips without breaking a rule of grammar, without showing in his dialect or brogue or uncouth tones his want of cultivation . . . cannot take the place to which perhaps his native good sense entitles him. To have intercourse with respectable people, we must speak their language" (*Self-Culture* 44–45).

This book is my attempt to "have intercourse with respectable people." But I want to map a position for myself somewhere between gentlemen (I refuse to be a gentle-lady) and the vulgar. Later, I discuss M. M. Bakhtin's notion of hybridization, but for now I will tell you that I consider myself an intentional hybrid. I am neither a flower (a gentleman) nor a weed (the vulgar). And if I had to choose between one or the other, frankly, I would choose to be a weed. Paulo Freire points out that one does not have to choose between "elitism" and "basism," and I would extend his statement. Neither does one have to choose between theory and practice, nor, despite what Matthew Arnold said, between culture and anarchy. So, while I will try not to break any rules of grammar, you may (if you are respectable) find me wanting in propriety, clearness, and grace. I hope I compensate for those "deficiencies" by clarifying the politics of those words as categories of evaluation.

The Culture Wars of the 1990s are the continuation of the struggle for real democracy that began in the eighteenth century, a struggle for unaristocratic and thus vulgar voices to be heard. The voices of the barbarous horde were silenced in eighteenth-century Scotland by Francis Hutcheson, Thomas Reid, Hugh Blair, and other philosophers and rhetoricians, and in nineteenth-century America by the Channings and their followers. More recently, attempts to silence the barbarous horde have been made by academics such as Allan Bloom and E. D. Hirsch, whose reactionary rhetoric borrows from classical rhetoric as well as the rhetoric of eighteenth-century Scots and nineteenth-century New Englanders. The irony is that the rhetoric the Scots devised as a way to modify traditional ideas came to be used by our contemporaries as a way to halt the flow of change. The once revolutionary rhetoric is now petrified as the rhetoric of reaction. This reactionary rhetoric perseveres most recently in Gertrude Himmelfarb's *The De-Moralization of Society* and James Q. Wilson's *The Moral Sense.*

I need to state here in unequivocal and vulgar terms that there is simply no such thing as the moral sense, a sense that is natural and universal, as Wilson argues. The truth is that the Scots, following Shaftesbury, made it up. They created it, named it, defined it, and explained how it worked, and, though it has undergone 250 years of modifications, some people still use the term exactly as the eighteenth-century Scottish philosophers used it. Throughout this book, I use the terms as the Scots and their rhetorical descendants used them, as well as the terms "man" or "men" as the writers at the time used them. Even though some scholars have argued that "man" or "men" were meant to include all people, they clearly were not. I use these exclusivist and masculinist forms to call attention to them rather than to indicate their referential accuracy. The Scots were ingenious. Considering "faculties" as real physical entities, they created a faculty, such as the moral sense or taste, whenever they needed it to explain some sort of human behavior, or rather, to define themselves as authorities on human behavior. A century later in the United States, primarily in the rhetoric of the Boston Unitarians, the language and concepts of the eighteenth-century Scots became reified. Now in the late twentieth century, the fabrications of the Scots enter our vocabulary as commonsensical presuppositions. Like retreads, their concepts are covered and put back on the road by the Right, whose political agenda includes—naturally—silencing the barbaric horde.

The ingenuity of the Scots is countered by the insidious effects of their rhetoric, as I hope to demonstrate. While I admire their creativity, I detest their absoluteness. Similarly, I admire the Boston Unitarians for asserting the ability of individuals to reason about their own morality and actions, but I hate their condescension. I love the four writers that I am primarily concerned with here—Ralph Waldo Emerson, James Russell Lowell, Oliver Wendell Holmes, and Thomas Wentworth Higginson—for trying to understand what was happening around them, and, even though it was too brief, for their participation in democratic action. But these men were snobs even by the standards of their time. Their Harvard and New England elitism blinded them, and the rhetoric they used to silence the barbaric horde deafened them. Unfortunately, it still blinds and deafens some of us.

Genteel Rhetoric

Introduction
Rhetoric and Culture

We all carry the Common in our heads as the unit of
space, the State House as the standard of architecture,
and measure off men in Edward Everetts as with a
yard-stick.
                                        —*Oliver Wendell Holmes*

In August of 1824, Edward Everett, orator, Harvard professor, editor of
North American Review, and statesman, delivered a Phi Beta Kappa address
entitled "The Circumstances Favorable to the Progress of Literature in America." Everett's listening audience that day was largely homogeneous—
male past and present members of Harvard's Phi Beta Kappa whom
Everett addressed as "brethren of one literary household" (9). This mode
of address, uttered then as a gesture toward inclusion, now calls attention
to itself. No doubt intended to put the audience in the "right frame of
mind" as Aristotle advised, the term now elicits questions: Who were
these brethren? What did they want? What have been the effects of their
desires on my life?

That Everett addressed members of his audience as "brethren of one literary household" indicates that he thought they would agree that America needed a literature of its own and that circumstances were indeed
favorable to its progress. And they did agree. Immediately after the Revolutionary War, the New England intelligentsia began to discuss establishing cultural independence through a uniquely American literature
that would be different from and better than literature from Europe.

In Massachusetts, the movement toward cultural autonomy took hold
simultaneously with the proliferation of print material. The first issue of
Boston Magazine, in 1783, announced that one-third of its pieces were written by Americans, and six years later the editors of *Massachusetts Magazine*
boasted that a majority of their authors were American. Noah Webster in-

sisted that "America must be as independent in literature as she is in politics." In part 1 of *A Grammatical Institute of the English Language* (1783), he wrote, "For America in her infancy to adopt the present maxims of the old world would be to stamp the wrinkles of decrepit age upon the bloom of youth and to plant the seeds of decay in a vigourous constitution." Using tropes of agedness to refer to England and Europe enabled Webster and others to juxtapose tropes of youth and originality when referring to America. We need to resort, Webster argued, to "original writers and original principles instead of taking upon trust what English writers please to give us" (qtd. in Spencer 26–28).

In the 1770s, as Gordon Wood has noted, describing England with metaphors of decrepitude and decay enabled colonists to develop an ideology of revolution (Wood 32). But fifty years after the Revolution, the metaphors remained. If England and Europe were timeworn, corrupt, decayed, and wrong, then America was new, pure, innocent, and right. Furthermore, with the conceptual model in place, creating a national literature became a patriotic imperative. To ensure themselves of America's independence and to establish its moral and cultural superiority, Americans had to write America. The term "America" generally was used by writers until well after the Civil War when the term "United States" came into vogue. Here I tend to use "America" as these writers used it because I want to mark the implicit imperialism in its use. The United States, after all, is only one area in the North American continent, and to its south is another continent that is also America, ideas that the early national writers failed to consider.

The infinite possibilities of writing America placed the writer in an "Adamic condition," a term used by the elder Henry James. Even as he uttered the words, however, James recognized the "sleek and comely Adamic condition" as remote from "human attributes" (Lewis 6). In other words, James understood that the "Adamic condition" as rhetorical situation was both blessing and curse. As the new Eden of the Puritans, America had accumulated a brief history, but as an independent nation it remained undefined and unwritten—a blank space, a cultural void. The need to give the new nation form and substance took on great urgency, but with the urgency of filling open space, as James understood, comes human frailty. While Everett, Webster, and others were calling upon Americans to write America, they wanted to be absolutely certain that the written America was better than the written Europe. The enormous responsibility of writing America required the right writing men. Though they sometimes figured the writer as Adam and American literature as original, they were not calling for innovative language and themes from unknown writers. On the contrary, American writing must come from men with cultural authority. Everett, a Greek scholar, looked to Greece for potential models.

"[T]he noble and elegant arts of Greece," he told the Phi Beta Kappans, sprang into life in a "region not unlike our own New England" (24). While in every new nation men's efforts understandably must be directed toward establishing government, that task is nearing completion in America, Everett observed, and therefore America's "cultivated talent" could now direct its energy toward letters. In matters of culture, Everett reminded his audience, Massachusetts had always led the way. "[W]here else in the world," Everett asked, "did the foundation of the college ever follow so closely on that of the republic, as in Massachusetts?" (16–17). In other words, men from Harvard were better prepared to write America than were other writers, a conclusion with which Everett's audience of literary brethren undoubtedly agreed.

Other Harvard men put forth the same argument but extended the area from Harvard to all of New England. Six years after Everett's speech, William Ellery Channing published in the *Christian Examiner* an essay entitled "Remarks on National Literature," in which he observed that the "mind" had converted "bleak and rock-bound New England" from a "wilderness into smiling fields and opulent cities," a transformation that furnished Channing with proof that when the "culture of man" is the goal, the "cultivation of nature" also becomes advanced (Robinson 169). Channing's linking of the terms "culture" and "cultivation" was not accidental. As did others of the Harvard elite, Channing conceived culture as a product of cultivation, and if the nation's literature would become the expression of superior minds, as Channing thought it should, then the writer necessarily must be cultivated. Thus the American writer was not an entirely innocent Adam, but rather Adam's self-conscious and highly perfected New England descendent.

Everett, Channing, and other learned New England men shared the same vision about what an American writer should be: moral and educated with an appreciation for proper art and literature, genteel in bearing and manners. William Ellery Channing argued that a national literature had "intimate connections with morals and religion, as well as with our public interests." For him a national literature meant the "expression of a nation's mind in writing" (Robinson 167). The writer not only would define America but in the process would define and exemplify the American man of letters. By naming and defining American literature and high culture, the writer could successfully claim the literary and cultural territory. Thus Harvard and New England claimed the territory of culture, morality, and taste.

Everett and Channing agreed that eminently qualified Harvard men should write the national literature and culture. And for the period immediately preceding the Civil War, this was indeed the case. In *New England Literary Culture,* Lawrence Buell notes that "Harvard was the region's chief literary breeding ground, attended by more than one-third of all male New England writers of consequence between the Revolution and the Civil War" (38). As Buell has demonstrated, writing in New England sprang from an oratorical culture grounded both in a governmental structure that encouraged public participation and in a Congregational tradition that placed high value upon an educated ministry. Buell acknowledges that the culture was elitist (138). At the risk of stating the obvious, I add that it was male.

Though both boys and girls could listen to sermons and certain ceremonial addresses such as those commemorating anniversaries of important events, addresses delivered on other occasions were not heard by women and girls. Certainly women were not Phi Beta Kappan literary brethren, nor were they exposed to formal rhetorical training. As Robert Connors points out, "[R]hetoric was a quintessentially *agonistic* discipline—concerned with contest." Because it was agonistic, it "reified in technical disciplinary form the sometimes inchoate agonistic longings of a patriarchal society" (67–68). Rhetoric, then—its study and its practice—was the domain of men.

Women might be "literary," as Harriet Beecher Stowe and other women writers later demonstrated, but they could not be "rhetorical." If women argued, their arguments had to be embedded in literature in ways that were less confrontive and more "feminine." Thus in *Uncle Tom's Cabin,* Stowe's strong arguments against the institution of slavery are embedded in her concerns for the institution of family, and the novel's major argument is that slavery destroys the family unit. Furthermore, while Connors is certainly right that rhetoric is a male domain, not all men could be rhetorical. In his work on Frederick Douglass, John Sekora notes that white abolitionists implored Douglass when he spoke publicly to only tell the story of his slavery and escape. In *My Bondage and My Freedom,* Douglass writes, "It did not entirely satisfy me to narrate wrongs; I felt like *denouncing* them" (qtd. in Sekora 610). Like Stowe, Douglass was permitted to operate in the narrative mode but not the rhetorical. Rhetoric was not the property of women and ex-slaves, though some, especially Douglass, stole it and put it to good use.

From the 1830s until after the Civil War, the privilege of public rhetorical authority came to be embodied within a certain group of men, the most authoritative of whom—those Buell refers to as "writers of consequence"—were schooled at Harvard under Boylston Professor of Rhetoric and Oratory Edward T. Channing. These young men also studied the sermons and lectures of Edward's brother William Ellery Channing as well as the speeches of Edward Everett. "Literature," as these men used the term, did not refer only to belletristic or imaginative writing. As William Ellery Channing put it, literature includes "all the writings of superior minds, be the subjects what they may" (Robinson 167). Thus conceived, literature was linked to the words of highly articulate men, whether they were speakers, writers, critics, or editors who wrote about science, history, belles lettres, morality, current events, or travel. Eventually, because of the spread of newspapers and magazines in the nineteenth century, the written word became the primary means of enculturation. But particularly in eastern Massachusetts, public address also was a significant means of spreading "literature." Thus Harvard men of letters wrote speeches, sermons, or lectures and read them to an audience or to several audiences. These oral addresses were reported in newspapers and then perhaps, if the speaker/writer had gained enough of a reputation, published as essays. Edward Everett, as a man of letters, wrote, published, and for a time edited the *North American Review,* but he also was a lyceum speaker, a professor, a senator, a governor, a university president, and an orator who earned the title the "Cicero of America." Ralph Waldo Emerson was one of his most ardent young devotees.

In 1880, two years before his death, Emerson delivered a lecture, which later became one of his most famous essays, entitled "Historic Notes of Life and Letters in New England." This lecture/essay purports to document the early influences on American Transcendentalism but actually documents early influences on Emerson. In this essay, Emerson mythicizes Everett as the American man of letters *par excellence* by referring to Everett as the "master of eloquence." What impressed Emerson was not so much Everett's words as his presentation: the "magic of form" and the "graces of manner." Emerson writes, "He had nothing in common with vulgarity and infirmity, but, speaking, walking, sitting, was as much aloof and uncommon as a star" (Miller 8–10).

While Emerson considered Everett's aloof and uncommon manner praiseworthy, to others Everett embodied snobbery. At the same time that Emerson and other Harvard men were writing their versions of the national literature, America was becoming a nation of industry and of immigrants. Immediately after the Revolution, agrarian America was still the symbol of virtue and freedom, but the same Enlightenment rationalism that promoted Revolutionary values also promoted the idea of progress in machine technology, and New England in particular surged toward modern industrial capitalism with its unequal distribution of wealth and power. No longer a provincial town where everyone knew everyone else, Boston and its surrounding area at mid-century contained over two hundred thousand people, many of them new immigrants eager to work in mills, factories, and railroads (Solomon 5). American literature, as envisioned by Everett and Channing, had little meaning for the immigrants, the poor, the factory workers, the farmers, the mechanics, the housewives, the cooks, the seamstresses. The newspapers and the popular press, more democratic in spirit, were more relevant to this segment of the population.

In 1857 an editorial writer for the New York *Herald* used Everett as an example of elitism. He wrote that since in America nobody has "superiors," the common man is "as good as Edward Everett." The editorial was prompted by the construction of New York's Central Park, designed to have a civilizing effect on the "uncivilized" masses. Its developer, Frederick Law Olmsted, had argued, "The poor need an education to refinement and taste and the mental and moral capital of gentlemen." Central Park, Olmsted believed, would provide "mental and moral capital" and would signify the "progress of art and esthetic culture in this country" (qtd. in Bushman 422).

While Olmsted hoped to refine the uncivilized through control and aestheticization of public space, other commercial-minded men promoted material forms of gentility: houses, furniture, carpets, paintings, and books, including, as John Kasson has shown, books on etiquette. Kasson ties the increasing market for etiquette books to the emergence of industrial capitalism and its interrelated developments—urbanization, transportation, and communication (*Rudeness* 35–43). These developments also created a refinement industry that produced, in addition to etiquette books, magazine articles and other instructional manuals for unschooled people who wanted to learn to speak and write correctly. Although members of this reading audience could not go to Harvard, Harvard writers could come to them through these publications.

Whereas Olmsted tried to produce refinement publicly, readers of books, magazines, and refinement manuals tried to consume it privately. But while readers could become more refined through private consumption, they could not become ultimately genteel. Commodities can be purchased and rules learned by reading books, but the gentility, the aloofness, the self-possession that Everett embodied as Emerson's "master of eloquence" could not be bought. Rather, one acquired the "graces of manner" and the "magic of form" by watching and listening and imitating. Gentility and eloquence are not so much learned as they are absorbed, and once absorbed, they are very powerful means of persuasion.

The French sociologist Pierre Bourdieu uses the term "habitus" to describe this kind of associational and tacit knowledge that serves as class conditioning. Bourdieu suggests that one's habitus becomes so internalized that it is written and can be read on the body. Once assimilated, habitus can then be turned to "cultural capital," a public and institutionalized set of practices or class markers used for social and cultural exclusion. Both habitus and cultural capital include not only the use of language but also attitudes, preferences, body language, and other kinds of behavior that may have use-value (*Distinction* 53, 54, 101). I argue here that the formal and informal knowledge the aspiring young writers attending Harvard absorbed enabled them to write a high literary and intellectual culture and to write themselves as members of that cultural elite. Their rhetoric created social reality.

Ronald Story, a social historian who studies antebellum Boston and Harvard, draws the distinction between "elite" and "upper class." According to Story, upper class "denotes a social elite which has achieved a singularly high degree of control, consciousness, and resolution," a position the elite of Boston did not achieve until 1870 (xii). Before about 1870 the class system was in flux. I will follow Story's categories and refer to the writers I discuss as "elite" rather than "upper-class." These writers did help to solidify the class system by using a rhetoric of high culture and by publicly evaluating their own culturally elite experiences as if they were natural and universal. About mid-century, for example, Oliver Wendell Holmes helped to establish the Boston and Harvard elite as upper-class by writing them into his novel *Elsie Venner* as "Brahmins."

Gregory Clark and Michael Halloran have argued that the rhetoric that preceded that of Holmes and his peers, that is, the neoclassical rhetoric as practiced by Edward Everett, enabled "citizens to think and act collectively beyond the boundaries of their professional subcultures" and enabled its practitioners to "articulate a public moral consensus" (24–25). Contemporary cultural criticism, however, indicates that the idea of a unified, monologic public consensus should be questioned. Consensus ideology assumes that ideas can be explained as commonly shared by all groups, but it ignores the power one group holds over another. Unproblematized, consensus imposes order without force; and by concealing hierarchical power structures, consensus benefits the privileged and powerful. Michel Foucault has shown that any discursive, textual, verbal practice always engages in the dissemination of power. It attempts to establish order and to create the things it names (see *The Order of Things*). When Edward Everett, standing before an audience of Phi Beta Kappans, called for a national literature, his words and manner in-formed the kind of literature he desired. If his audience of literary brethren could absorb and use some of Everett's manner, that is, absorb the habitus he embodied, then they too could become agents of high culture or, to use Bourdieu, high-cultural capitalists.

If highly trained orators like Everett were successful because they were able to articulate a consensus, as Halloran and Clark argue, the consensus they articulated was restricted to those who admired erudition, belletrism, and gentility. These listeners received Everett and his message positively because, like Emerson, they valued both his experience and his aloofness and wanted to re-create it. Instead of characterizing their response as consensual, I would argue that their positive reception was a product of their desire to be, or to be like, Edward Everett. The writing of the men who answered Everett's call for an American literature was an expression of their desire to reproduce Everett by producing themselves as American men of letters.

Everett's rhetoric had a certain familiar ring to literary brethren schooled in the classics. It was a particular strand of classical rhetoric adapted by Christianity that George Kennedy and other historians of rhetoric call "sophistic." Stemming from the rhetoric of the Greek Sophists, this rhetoric typically does not deal with difficult decisions. Rather than being deliberative, forensic, or argumentative, it is ceremonial, moral, and literary (17). The persuasive power of this strand of rhetoric is anthropocentric. In the *Antidosis* Isocrates argues that a man becomes virtuous by contemplating and imitating other great men. While this notion appears straightforward, it is not innocent nor unproblematic. Consider the kind of rhetorical culture this rhetoric might create. If virtue is learned and rhetoric practiced by devoted imitation, then cultural heroes perpetually become reproduced and their ideas reified.

This strand of rhetoric was extended in Rome by Cicero and Quintilian, who taught that only good men become good orators. The anthropocentric rhetorical theory of Cicero and Quintilian blended oratorical skill and moral purpose, with Quintilian defining oratory as the "good man speaking well." The "perfect orator," Quintilian argues, "cannot exist unless he is first a good man." Quintilian requires of this orator "not only a consummate ability in speaking, but also every excellence of mind" (6). "Excellence of mind" requires the right kind of educational and social nurturance for its formation. Like Edward Everett's aloofness, it cannot be learned superficially.

Because this rhetoric stressed the moral training of young men, early Christians found it easily adaptable to their purposes, and thus the civic virtue embodied in the Greek and Roman orator became Christian virtue as embodied in the preacher. As Kennedy points out, the word for "preach" in Mark 13:10 is *kerusso*, which literally means "proclaim" (127). The Christian address or sermon is a proclamation whose authority is based on Christian grace, a certain kind of ethical appeal that removes itself from demonstration or logic. Particularly in America with its strong

Calvinist-Puritan tradition, public speeches such as Everett's, which typically contained biblical references, more closely resembled the Christian sermon than the Greek or Roman declamation. The rhetorical authority that Emerson described as "graces of manner" derives not so much from words (logos) as from identity and character (ethos), an ethos that blends the sophistic and Christian traditions and enables the speaker or writer, by virtue of who he is, to proclaim. In Everett's time and place, this kind of rhetorical authority or cultural capital came from being male, Anglo-Saxon, elite, and Harvard-educated, with further education in divinity or law preferred.

After graduating first in his class in 1811, Everett was encouraged by his mentor, the young liberal minister Joseph Stevens Buckminster, to attend Harvard Divinity School. Upon graduation, he was offered the pulpit in Boston's prestigious Brattle Street Church. The next year Harvard offered him a professorship in Greek and sent him to Europe to study. Though Everett welcomed the opportunity to study in Europe and seemed glad to leave the pulpit, he wrote his brother Alexander that he felt a "strong attachment to the act of preaching" (qtd. in Varg 19). Everett found that as a professor he could proclaim/profess without the social restrictions imposed on a minister, and, if we believe Emerson, the young men at Harvard proved to be devoted imitators.

In his history of Harvard, Samuel Eliot Morison credits Everett and Edward Tyrell Channing with creating the "classic New England diction—the measured, dignified speech, careful enunciation, precise choice of words, and well-modulated voice" (216). Although Morison seems to be discussing speech, I take his term "classic New England diction," to refer not only to spoken but also to written words. Both Everett and Edward T. Channing assumed their teaching duties at Harvard in 1819, Everett as professor of Greek and Channing as Boylston Professor of Rhetoric and Oratory. Everett taught at Harvard only five years. After serving in the House of Representatives, he served four terms as governor of Massachusetts, returned to Harvard as president from 1846 to 1849, then became a senator.

Edward T. Channing, on the other hand, remained at Harvard for thirty-two years, and during those years he taught rhetoric to many young men who later established themselves as American men of letters, shapers of what literary historians have called the New England Renaissance. These men included Emerson, Henry David Thoreau, Oliver Wendell Holmes, James Russell Lowell, Thomas Wentworth Higginson, Richard Henry Dana, Jr., Charles Eliot Norton, Edward Everett Hale, and others. Edward T. Channing's rhetorical theory is neither original nor redundant and neither classical nor Romantic. It is, rather, genteel. Edward

Channing is a significant figure in the history of American rhetoric primarily because of his famous students, and his *Lectures Read to the Seniors at Harvard College* are important because they indicate what he said to the young men who became major contributors to the New England Renaissance. Channing's rhetorical pedagogy, his vocabulary and concepts, enabled these young men to represent themselves as American writers of high culture and to establish Boston as the center of high culture.

From its beginning in 1636 Harvard had a relationship with Boston that can best be described as symbiotic. Historically, Boston's merchants had been Harvard's chief benefactors; for example, the Boston merchants Thomas Hancock and Nicholas Boylston both endowed important chairs, the latter occupied by Edward T. Channing. In return, Harvard provided Boston with learned graduates, especially graduates to fill its pulpits. Lewis Simpson notes that around 1800 Harvard graduates filled the pulpits of Boston's First Church, King's Chapel, Brattle Street Church, New South Church, Federal Street Church, Hollis Street Church, and West Church (497–98). Some Harvard graduates, instead of becoming ministers or men of letters, chose to become bankers, lawyers, or insurance brokers. Others became entrepreneurs, engaging in maritime commerce, textile manufacturing, and railroads (Story 4). As Ronald Story points out, the development of a capitalist upper class in Boston involved the consolidation of group interests—an integration of potentially rival factions, a harmonizing of business and cultural elements, and an elaboration of a coherent value system (Story 6–7). The economic and social link between Harvard and Boston helped to shape the preachers, teachers, and writers I discuss in this study. They in turn helped to shape Boston's high culture by speaking and writing about it in rhetoric that was epideictic and quasireligious.

In his lecture/essay "Boston," Ralph Waldo Emerson writes unironically, "I do not speak with any fondness, but the language of coldest history, when I say that Boston commands attention as the town which was appointed in the destiny of nations to lead the civilization of North America" (*Complete Works* 12:90). Emerson's statement is typical of his generation of writers who hyperbolically praised Boston for its high culture. This rhetoric, repeated through generations, began with John Winthrop's 1630 sermon aboard the *Arabella.* Winthrop told the first colonists of the Massachusetts Bay Colony that they would establish a city upon a hill with the eyes of all people upon them. Since Winthrop's sermon, the idea of the city upon a hill was perpetuated until Boston became a mythical city blessed by God. In the nineteenth century the myth was reified in confident expressions such as Emerson's and in the writing of Emerson's younger contemporaries, particularly Oliver Wendell Holmes, who peopled the mythical Boston with "Brahmins," the "untitled aristocracy" which produces "races of scholars" (*Elsie Venner* 4). As poet, novelist, essayist, medical doctor, and son of Harvard, Oliver Wendell Holmes, like Emerson, held enough rhetorical authority so that what he wrote about Boston was cultural capital both for Boston and himself.

The writing that came from the Boston area in the nineteenth century was characterized by a later generation as genteel. Harvard philosophy professor George Santayana coined the phrase "genteel tradition" in his 1911 address entitled "The Genteel Tradition in American Philosophy." For Santayana, Harvard and Boston were sites of great conflict, but having graduated from Harvard and taught there, he, like Holmes and other Harvardians, used these particular sites to generalize about the nation. Santayana characterized the United States as a "young country with an old mentality" or rather, "it is a country with two mentalities, one a survival of the belief and standards of the fathers, the other an expression of the instincts, practice, and discoveries of the younger generations. In all the higher things of the mind—in religion, in literature, in the moral emotions—it is the hereditary spirit that still prevails" (D. Wilson 39). Santayana describes the genteel half of the American mind not so much "high-and-dry" as "slightly becalmed; it has floated gently in the backwater, while alongside, in invention and industry and social organization the other half of the mind was leaping down a sort of Niagara Rapids" (D. Wilson 40). For Santayana Boston was a microcosm of the entire country whose intellect was split between what was inherited from Europe or from the Puritans and what was to be invented or discovered.

By developing a schizophrenic model of America, Santayana at least acknowledges conflicts and discontinuities whereas other thinkers, particularly social and cultural historians, often use the word "transformation" to describe rapid changes in ideas and practices during the nineteenth century. Historians of American rhetoric have tended to do the same. Thus James Berlin argues that after the Civil War American colleges were "transformed," becoming more democratic and less elitist, more committed to science, business, and industry and less committed to religion. Changes in curriculum, Berlin argues, necessarily brought about transformations in rhetorical theory, removing from its realm ethical and moral concerns as well as the classical notion of discovery and emphasizing instead a "managerial invention" that focuses on audience rather than on the speaker/writer or on the content (*Writing Instruction* 58–65).

In a similar vein Gregory Clark and Michael Halloran maintain that the authority of the early-nineteenth-century orator, based in civic and consensus-building rhetoric, was "transformed by an emerging individualist spirit." Subsequently, the rise of professionalism toward the end of the nineteenth century resulted in the transformation of the authority of the individual into the authority of experts. Clark and Halloran call their study of nineteenth-century oratory a "historiography of transformation" that commits them to "acknowledge losses and gains" (3–5). I would argue that the word "transformation" suggests an evolutionary development that is continuous and complete. It ignores or evades jumps, false starts, discontinuities, or resistance.

In discussions of nineteenth-century rhetoric "transformation" may be useful as a methodological term, yet it sometimes oversimplifies a complex process. To say that one thing becomes another thing like a caterpillar becomes a butterfly ignores that within the butterfly much of the caterpillar is still intact. Further, I would argue that the minds of writers I describe here, at least as indicated by their rhetoric, are not so neatly divided as Santayana's model. While they assimilated Boston/Harvard traditions as habitus, they were also intellectuals who responded to new ideas, new events, and new social situations. As a result, they produced a body of rhetoric that is both conflicted and confluent. Their discourse is complicated further by their desires to become representative voices, prophets of high American culture.

I will examine this rhetoric as it was practiced in its vicissitudes, that is, within its cultural context. This work is meant to be both a rhetorical history and a cultural study. I deliberately exclude transformative models and comparative models. When I use dualist models, I do so only to point to sites of conflict and resistance. To perceive this rhetoric as simply inherited, created, or transformed is, I believe, to evade the issues of its time and the concerns of these writers.

I will also place this rhetoric within its political and economic contexts. At the time these writers lived and wrote, the young republic was claiming to be a democracy; yet while republicans extolled abstract egalitarian ideals such as "equal justice," a glance around them revealed the materiality of poverty and exploitation. Most important, embedded within the ideal republic was the material institution of slavery, an institution whose reality finally became such a crucial moral issue that even the most reticent genteel writer had to confront it. I will explore how slavery and the impending national crisis collided with the literary concerns of these teachers, preachers, and writers.

The growth of a capitalist economy between 1830 and 1860 impelled Americans to seek the exchange of goods and ideas for private profit. Capitalist values and the rhetoric of the marketplace seeped into genteel rhetoric sometimes without its practitioners' awareness. Sometimes these writers articulated capitalist expansion and entrepreneurship as national progress, at other times as individual selfishness. During this period, the spread of capitalist enterprise, the institutionalization of literary and cultural criticism, the establishment of class hierarchies, and the politics of slavery were interconnected. Rather than focusing on changes in rhetorical theory or practice, I want to study ways that ideological and material issues intruded on the genteel discursive practices of these writers as they attempted to define and exemplify high American culture.

In its broadest sense this study explores the relation between social structures and public discourse or, more simply, between ways of living and ways of writing. In practicing their craft, writers necessarily assume social roles. These roles can be described in a purely theoretical way as subject positions. The writing subject is *subject to* a particular social reality—convention, custom, history, tradition. As a result, his or her writing is in a sense determined or at least circumscribed by historical conditions, including language conventions. In this theoretical case, the discourse the subject produces actually reproduces the social structures already in place. As reproducers of social structures writers sustain continuity and legitimize power relations. These reproducers can be figured as Santayana's "becalmed" mind. But writing subjects rarely are totally passive receivers of historical conditions. Unless what they write is banal, they are also actors, doers, agents who create a new idea, say something in a new way, modify conventional language, challenge power relations, disrupt continuity. When writers change, modify, or create new meanings, their personal organization changes also. The "self" they had written earlier is not the "self" they are now writing. Most writers ignore the problem; either they are unaware of it, or they hope nobody else will notice. Others acknowledge it with statements such as Walt Whitman's "Do I contradict myself? Very well, then, I contradict myself."

These two theoretical cases of the writing subject, dualist and structural, are useful only as a descriptive starting point, and if left there, the writer's "self," like Santayana's American mind, is hopelessly schizophrenic. Writers, however, do not function as either passive/determined or active/creative. Rather, they function as both, and, as a result, they are constantly creating a new writing "self." Yet they continue to write within a constructed range of possibilities inscribed within them as well as within their social world. The "self" the writer creates whenever he or she challenges tradition or convention is not a "transformed self" in the sense that it is new or complete; rather, the writer's "self" constantly breaks apart and undergoes accommodations and adaptations. The men whose writing I discuss here conserve some traditional ideas and structures; their words are the product of a way of thinking of which they were not original producers. Yet often these writers try to effect change, to become themselves primary producers. Throughout, they use writing as an act of asserting their writer's authority, as self-authorization. The authorizing voices these writers use to discuss literature and high culture, however, break apart when they write about material issues, particularly those of slavery and war. Acutely aware of the problems of the coherent "self," Emerson solved the problem by embracing inconsistency. Other writers were not so brave or foolish.

I study the writing of these men to find out how they authorized themselves to produce texts, how they manipulated European neoclassical and belletristic ideas and language, what happened to their voices as they dealt with slavery, abolition, and the Civil War. I am working within a selective tradition, a rhetoric pared down to selected documents of specific writers—in other words, a rhetorical culture. The center of this rhetorical culture was Harvard College; its expanse included the lecturing and writing environment first in the Boston area, later other places that sponsored lecture series, and finally, the reading audience of magazines such as the *Atlantic Monthly*. The questions I ask are the following: Under what conditions and to what ends did this rhetoric emerge? How was it used to inculcate characteristics advantageous to its practitioners? That is, what were the hegemonic practices of this group of writers? How were those hegemonic practices called into question first by the possibility then by the reality of abolition and war?

Because I argue that what is taught in classrooms, that is, pedagogic action, provides only part of the rhetorical training for young orators or writers, the bulk of my source material is not strictly pedagogical. Though I begin with the textbook rhetoric of Edward T. Channing's *Lectures Read to the Seniors at Harvard College*, I use it dialectically in order to converse between Edward Channing's rhetorical pedagogy and the rhetorical practices of his brother William Ellery Channing, influential Boston minister and major definer of American Unitarianism. Then I move from the classroom and pulpit into the essays of four of E. T. Channing's students: Ralph Waldo Emerson, Oliver Wendell Holmes, James Russell Lowell, and Thomas Wentworth Higginson, all of whom were major contributors to premier New England magazines such as *North American Review* and *Atlantic Monthly*, where Lowell served also as editor. Because these writers were at Harvard during the high tide of Unitarianism and either were themselves Unitarian ministers or had fathers who were ministers, they necessarily were influenced by liberal Christian ideas and Scottish Enlightenment language that combined with other currents such as federalism and republicanism. The rhetoric of the Scottish Enlightenment had been influenced by Calvinist theology not only indirectly by time and place, but also directly, since, excepting Adam Smith and David Hume, all the major figures of the Enlightenment in Scotland were ministers. These eighteenth-century ministers/rhetoricians as well as the nineteenth-century Harvard writers understood that combining various strains of thought was a useful rhetorical strategy.

In his essay "Revisionary Histories of Rhetoric," James Berlin calls for a kind of revisionary rhetorical history that uses interdisciplinary methods, explores culture in its expansive formulation, and offers a nontotalizing narrative that examines discourse, social interactions, social structures, ideologies, and modes of production (112–27). I attempt here this type of study, using cultural theory, social theory, postcolonial theory, feminist theory, and rhetorical theory to examine writers at work in their particular time and place and to formulate my reactions and inventions as reader. I rely on particular theorists whose work is not definitive, but instead is evocative and heuristic.

The term "culture" is used here in two senses. The first, "high culture," can be defined as Matthew Arnold's defined "culture" in *Culture and Anarchy*: the "best that has been thought and said in the world" (6). This definition assumes that culture is a standard that can be rated by absolute and universal values. The men whose writing I discuss held this nineteenth-century view of culture, a view that links culture with cultivation and thus holds culture captive to the judgments of the elite who determine what is the best. My notion of culture follows that of Raymond Williams. That is, culture is a social construct describing a particular way of life (41). In order to analyze culture from this perspective, one looks at historical, social, and institutional structures as well as means of production and reproduction—texts or other media. In this study nineteenth-century texts provide the rhetoric whose context is history and society.

Now a word about myself as reader. An audience created out of print technology distant in time and place from the original words may turn out to be troublesome for the writer. That these particular writers often published their lectures as essays and compiled their essays as books indicates their desire for eventual remote readers. They were acutely aware that a reading audience provided the potential for wider and more enduring fame. But later generations, particularly those of us trying to write histories from earlier print sources, may not be kind to writers whose reputations were based on a certain kind of writing "self" embodied as the erudite word written with the patrician hand. I study these writers not from the privileged position of disinterested observer but more aptly as a guest, who, though she may have been invited, nevertheless feels a bit ill at ease in the company of these nineteenth-century, Harvard-educated, male luminaries. And I am a guest with an agenda.

While it is true that I am an academic and white, a fact that affords me a certain access, I am also a woman, a single mother, a product of the working class, and a feminist. I have learned too much about nineteenth-century patriarchy to dismiss the knowledge that women provided comfortable writing environments for these writers—by keeping the children quiet, by uttering encouraging words, sometimes by using their inherited capital to enable the male writer to abandon another career. Often these women provided even more concrete assistance. Elizabeth Peabody, for example, copied the illegible words of William Ellery Channing's sermons and carried the text to the printer. Thomas Wentworth Higginson acknowledges that his sister "wrote for me all the passages that were found worth applauding" in his commencement oration (*Cheerful Yesterdays* 17). One wonders what else she wrote for him. When her father began to grow senile, Ellen Emerson stitched together the pages of his manuscript so he wouldn't lose his way among the pages as he lectured. As Perry Miller notes, she also helped him piece together publishable manuscripts from "older jottings" (Miller 3). What exactly does "piece together" mean? The general encouraging and enabling as well as the specific copying, stitching, and piecing are signifying practices as much as the text on the page—practices, as James Berlin notes, that "are always at the center of conflict and contention" ("Poststructuralism" 139). But in the writing situations I examine, the female scribes and stitchers remain shadow-dwellers while the male writers name, define, control, and affix their names to the text. My reference point necessarily is the text, and it is within the text that I begin my interrogation.

The questions I ask of texts, however, are constituted by my life experiences, and the answers I invent help to constitute my writing self or selves. As I write, I negotiate the two theoretical writing subjects I discussed earlier. That is, "I" am determined by the texts, by academic writing conventions, by traditional rhetorical criticism, as "I" interrogate and challenge them. At certain junctures, "I" submit and obey, but at other times, "I" contend and defy. Sometimes my defiance is what William Ellery Channing called "vulgar." At other times it borrows the language of neo-Marxist cultural criticism that, because it is theoretical, is at least as erudite as, and often more opaque than, the genteel rhetoric I am examining. My readers, I hope, will understand the complexity and irony of my rhetorical situation and bear with me as I move among writing selves.

In *The Practice of Everyday Life*, Michel de Certeau discusses what he calls "strategic" rhetorical models. According to de Certeau, a strategic model is possible when a "place can be circumscribed as *proper*" (his italics) and can "serve as the basis for generating relations with an exterior distinct from it" (xix). In this case the strategic model I have chosen to investigate is a rhetoric of high culture. Its proper place is a long way from my conservative upbringing in central Kentucky; from my first teaching position, at an all-black junior high school located in the middle of two housing projects; and from my present campus in the urbanized Arizona desert. It is the environment of nineteenth-century male Harvardians who lived in or close to Boston and who had family or social connections that placed them within Holmes's "Brahmin caste." Though I insert myself within their proper place in order to question and to form my interpretations, I deliberately choose to remain at the exterior.

1

Teaching and Preaching Culture and Character

No empire is so valuable as the empire of one's self.
—William Ellery Channing

A man's mind is known by the company it keeps.
—James Russell Lowell

When George Washington presented his Farewell Address to the cabinet in 1796, he stressed the need to stabilize the young and fragile government of the United States whose strength was the Constitution. Citizens, he said, should "resist with care the spirit of innovation" upon the Constitution since to alter it would be to "impair the energy of the system." Time and habit, Washington said, are "necessary to fix the true character of governments," for which "religion and morality are indispensable supports." Without religion, there is no "security for property, for reputation, for life," and morality simply "cannot endure without religion" (Ravitch 38–39).

In the view of Washington and other Federalists, the state operated like the human body whose energy, efficiency, and moral integrity were sustained through adherence to order and habit. From the Puritans the Federalists inherited missionary rhetoric and myth—America as a great mission and Americans as God's chosen. Sacvan Bercovitch has pointed out that missionary rhetoric was broad enough to "facilitate the transitions from Puritan to Yankee, and from errand to manifest destiny and the dream" (35). The Federalists' mission was to achieve perfection in government by putting in place a structure whose leaders were enlightened, well-educated men of character, political versions of the Puritan Saint or the Calvinist Elect. As Washington indicated, perfection of government relied on perfection of individuals. Washington's address served to caution younger Americans against the dangers of innovation and irreligion, factors that destabilized the body politic.

As the new nation's first president, Washington was the embodiment of the Federalist missionary, the Great Father, whose voice advises, admonishes, sanctions, warns, and compels. While the rhetorical authority of such a voice derives partially from its paternal words and demeanor, in order to have its desired effect the father's authority must be legitimized. In other words, fathers need sons. And indeed Washington's rhetoric produced sons who reproduced him as the nation's father. Daniel Webster, for example, observed that Washington's address represented the "highest character of truly disinterested, sincere, parental advice" (77).

Two years after Washington's Farewell Address, Harvard's Hasty Pudding Club toasted Washington's birthday as follows: "GEORGE WASHINGTON, a man brave without temerity, laborious without ambition, generous without prodigality, noble without pride, and virtuous without severity" (qtd. in Morison 186). The young Harvardians celebrated their roles as sons by characterizing Washington in a rhetoric as perfectly balanced as the "father" they were reproducing. Years later when Edward Tyrell Channing wrote about his grandfather William Ellery, signer of the Declaration of Independence, he described Ellery's character in similar terms. Men such as Ellery, he wrote, possess an "invisible virtue," that inspires the young with "prudence and self-respect, and a sense of justice and decency, and thus gradually [gives] a tone to manners and opinions in the neighborhood." Such men as Ellery, his grandson wrote, may leave their families and neighbors to serve a larger public, but they remain virtually unchanged ("Life" 87–88).

Like George Washington and other Founding Fathers, William Ellery became a mythical hero, invented and described as stable, ordered, balanced, and impartial. Continually reproduced as fortification against populism and democracy, these mythical fathers protected the sons against the unstable and passionate Jeffersonians or Jacksonians. In *The Organization of American Culture,* Peter Dobkin Hall notes that because the republic needed to be secured institutionally, the will of the individual Founding Fathers eventually gave way to corporations that privileged the wealthy and the educated. These corporations were as paternalistic as the Fathers by acting in what they defined as public interest (80–81). Another means of incorporation is the written reproduction of the Founding Fathers.

Impelled into public life reluctantly, the Fathers, so those who wrote about them would have us believe, treated the affairs of the nation and its lawmakers in the same detached and fair manner as they treated the affairs and members of their household. According to Edward Channing, his grandfather considered his public obligations as "high as those that bound him to his wife and children" ("Life" 106). Like the home, the state was the "object of affection." Grandfather Ellery was the family man called to public duty who "never changed with his condition or duties" and whose "interest was wholly moral" ("Life" 107). In Edward Channing's words, he had an "imperishable power of character" ("Life" 88).

The same "power of character" used to describe the Founding Fathers became a major theme in the lectures on rhetoric Edward Channing presented to seniors at Harvard during his tenure as Boylston Professor of Rhetoric and Oratory, from 1819 to 1851. In this chapter I inspect the "power of character" as it was used as a major persuasive technology in the nineteenth-century rhetoric of Edward Channing and that of his brother William Ellery Channing, Unitarian minister and public lecturer. The sources of this rhetoric of character can be traced through the neoclassical philosophy and rhetoric of the Scottish Enlightenment. Borrowing from classical and neoclassical ideas and merging these ideas with themes within federalism and Unitarianism, the Channing brothers produced an American rhetoric of high culture, an institutional and social text whose persuasive authority relied on knowledge, style, and charisma, or what Bourdieu calls "habitus."

Even before he assumed his professorship at Harvard, Edward Tyrell Channing was known as the grandson of the famous signer of the Declaration of Independence. The family, extended by in-laws, included Massachusetts Chief Justice Francis Dana and the celebrated painter Washington Allston. The most distinguished member of the immediate family was William Ellery Channing, a liberal minister who had served Boston's Federal Street Church since 1803. William graduated from Harvard in 1798, returned there to study theology, and later served on its governing board, the Harvard Corporation. Highly visible as a public man, William was active on various committees at Harvard, including a committee that judged student essays.

Unlike his older brother William, Edward did not graduate with his class at Harvard. He began there in 1804, but in 1807 he and his younger brother Walter were sent home and deprived of their degrees for taking part in a student rebellion. Nevertheless, Edward went on to practice law and to edit for a short time the *North American Review,* the premier New England magazine of literature and opinion. In 1819, the year he assumed the Boylston chair, Harvard awarded him an honorary M.A. This was also the year that William Ellery Channing preached his famous "Baltimore Sermon" that set forth the tenets of Unitarianism, earned him the leadership of the Unitarian movement, and alarmed and dismayed traditional Calvinists.

Unitarians had gained control of Harvard in 1805 with Henry Ware's election as Hollis Professor of Divinity. A combination of Protestant and Enlightenment ideas, Unitarianism stressed rationality in religion and freedom of conscience, both concepts strongly opposed to orthodox Calvinist theology. Daniel Walker Howe and other historians of American religion argue that the foundation for American Unitarianism was primarily the philosophy of the eighteenth-century Scottish Enlightenment, usually referred to as Common Sense philosophy (D. Howe 5). The so-called Common Sense philosophers of the Scottish Enlightenment typically were Moderate Calvinist ministers in the Church of Scotland. Francis Hutcheson and Thomas Reid articulated the philosophy, which George Campbell and Hugh Blair incorporated into their rhetoric texts.

Following the Scots and opposing the stern dogma of Puritan Calvinism, the Harvard Unitarians dispensed with thorny theological issues and instead emphasized ethics, an emphasis that insisted that "a man is not a Christian in proportion to the amount of truth he puts into *creed,* but in proportion to the amount of truth he puts into his *life*" (qtd. in D. Howe 7). In other words, Unitarianism emphasized character rather than belief.

In order to demonstrate high moral character, Unitarians insisted upon behavior and action in the world of affairs. Yet Unitarianism was never a populist religion. As a matter of fact, it frowned upon evangelical, fundamentalist religious expression. Unitarianism's "neighborhood," as historians have reminded us, was Boston, its center was Harvard, and its appeal was to an educated elite. Though its ministers and teachers spoke in universal terms, their views were those of a highly select elite culture. When Edward Channing used the term "power of character" to describe his grandfather and other Founding Fathers, he referred to an exclusive group of men.

Though they considered themselves the vanguard of liberal Christianity, in politics the Boston and Harvard Unitarians were Federalists and later Whigs. Harvard's historian Samuel Eliot Morison notes that as early as 1794 "the economic ruling class of New England" lined up with "Washington, Adams, and Hamilton in vigorous opposition to French Jacobinism and its American apologists" (185). In America "Jacobinism" referred to any form of political turbulence but was used especially to refer to the advocacy of popular democracy, politics as practiced first by the followers of Thomas Jefferson and later those of Andrew Jackson. In the late eighteenth century, the American Federalists used the excesses of the French Revolution as frightening examples of what could happen with the collapse of a strong central government whose pillars—embodied in America in the mythicized Founding Fathers—were stability, harmony, and order. Federalists perceived themselves not only as guardians of stable government but also as standard-bearers of universal moral sense.

In 1798 when young William Ellery Channing was elected commencement orator, Harvard's faculty had prohibited political discussion, a prohibition prompted by the previous year's commencement where young orators, inflamed with federalism, railed against Jeffersonians. William and other class members considered the ban on political discussion an infringement of free speech, but after offering to resign as class orator, William was persuaded to deliver his oration and avoid the topic of politics, particularly the mention of the French Revolution. William concluded his address with the statement, "But that I am forbid, I could a tale unfold, which would harrow up your souls" (W. H. Channing 72). The audience, of course, knew the tale. By employing this shrewd rhetorical tactic, William managed to allude to the forbidden topic without actually mentioning it. William's facility with language eventually earned him a reputation as the leading spokesman not only for Unitarianism but, in a more general way, for New England public morality.

Like other sons of Washington, William Ellery Channing perceived the French Revolution as a signifying force. Years later when reflecting on his college years, William wrote, "College was never in a worse state than when I entered it. Society was passing through a most critical stage. The French Revolution had diseased the imagination and unsettled the understanding of men everywhere. The old foundations of social order, loyalty, tradition, habit, reverence for antiquity, were everywhere shaken, if not subverted. The authority of the past was gone" (W. H. Channing 60).

Ironically, as the major definer of American Unitarianism, William could subvert the authority of traditional Calvinism, but as a Federalist and a son and grandson of Federalists, he believed that without respect for social stability, the government of the young nation would crumble as quickly as the *ancien regime* had crumbled in France. The "spirit of innovation" that Washington had cautioned against in his Farewell Address was the enemy of social and governmental stability. After the Hartford Convention in 1804, the Federalist party waned and eventually dissolved, yet loyalty to conservative Federalist ideals persisted at Harvard and in Boston. These ideals—order, harmony, stability, and impartiality in individuals and in the body politic—became embedded in the rhetoric of both Edward Tyrell Channing and William Ellery Channing. An individual, always male, who embodied these attributes could be described as possessing "power of character."

In his brief biography of Edward Channing, his nephew Richard Henry Dana, Jr., states that Channing "was educated in the school of Washington, and adopted the opinions of the Federal party." Dana explains that Edward Channing's Federalist opinions made him a "conservative, in the true and high sense of that term" (xvi). Channing's conservatism compelled him to pass on to his students certain beliefs about the relationships between moral rectitude and public communication. These beliefs can be subsumed under the term Edward used to describe his grandfather: power of character. In rhetorical history "power of character" is associated with Ciceronian rhetoric, particularly the notion that in order to become an orator or writer, one had to first become a good man.

In *De Inventione,* Cicero wrote that to neglect the study of philosophy and moral conduct while studying oratorical principles is a dangerous practice. When men acquired the power of eloquence without learning moral duty, Cicero argued, the result was corruptness in individuals, in society, and in government (3–7). Edward Channing was an admirer of Cicero and Cicero's rhetorical successor Quintilian, who outlined a pedagogy designed to produce the good man. Throughout his thirty-one years of teaching, Edward Channing taught that the right sort of education and moral training was a necessary condition to becoming a public speaker and writer. And in fact, since Harvard had been founded by Puritans, its teachers had always paid attention to students' morality, and students understood this attention as part of their education. In 1721, for example, the resident fellows wrote that the aim of the college was "Learned and pious Education of Youth, their Instruction in Languages, arts, and sciences, and having their minds and manners form'd aright" (qtd. in Morison 22–23). Edward Channing's lectures on rhetoric with their emphasis on moral character, therefore, fell within the tradition established two centuries earlier by Harvard's Puritan founders. But because of New England's expanding print technology and capitalist economy, nineteenth-century Harvard graduates had the potential to become more widely influential and wealthier than their Puritan forefathers.

Ronald Story notes that in Boston by 1860 the top one percent of the adult population owned two-fifths of the taxable wealth. As they became wealthier, Bostonians devoted their time and capital to permanent high cultural institutions such as Harvard College, the Boston Athenaeum, the Lowell Institute, the Massachusetts Historical Society, and the American Academy of Arts and Letters. All but Harvard appeared between the end of the Revolutionary War and 1840, and all were heavily endowed by Bostonians. The Boston elite generated wealth through their entrepreneurial spirit and conserved it through marriage and through institutional establishment. As these institutions developed, they became agents of class coherence (Story 3–9). The symbiotic relationship between Boston and Harvard meant that most of Boston's wealthy families sent their sons to Harvard, and these Harvard graduates in turn "pursued increasingly secular and business-oriented careers, lived in increasingly affluent styles, and possessed increasingly large estates" (Story 96).

Within Boston's and Harvard's elite culture during the first half of the nineteenth century, ideas and vocabulary from the Scottish Enlightenment combined with those of a declining federalism and an emerging Unitarianism to form a particular New England rhetoric that emphasized moral character, education, and aesthetics. Both Edward and William Ellery Channing, as influential teacher and preacher, taught and practiced this rhetoric and provided young men with an operational logic and vocabulary useful to them as writers of American literature and morality.

Rather than separating rhetoric from the rhetor by assigning to it a set of external rules, Edward Channing places rhetorical authority within the mind and heart—the character—of the speaker or writer. Agreeing with Cicero and Quintilian that rhetoric, or as Channing sometimes called it, "eloquence," is a powerful force that holds the potential to serve good or evil, Channing believed that the speaker or writer necessarily had to be moral. But mere morality was not enough. For Channing, morality was linked to education defined as mastery of knowledge and mastery of emotions. Following the tradition of Cicero and Quintilian, Edward Channing argued that a classical education in the liberal arts best suited a man for the work of life. "The aim of a liberal education," he argued, "is not to fit a man for a particular calling . . . but to give him a ready command of all faculties and strengthen them to the utmost; so that he shall come to his profession with a general invigoration and flexibility which prepare him for the study of any." Similarly, a rhetorical education should include not only attention to oratory, "but all departments of literature" so that the student can "obtain a mastery of all its principles to serve any occasion" (*Lectures* 39). The use of masculinist metaphors—"command," "strengthen," "mastery"—serve as a reminder that a rhetorical education not only was not for women, but also not for fainthearted men. In Edward Channing's Federalist mind, speaking or writing in public was the realm of the strong, stable, impartial male. Before he can "bring men to [his] way of thinking," and "make them act according to [his] wishes," which Channing says is the object of rhetoric (*Lectures* 13), a man must first master the knowledge a liberal education provides, and in the process, master his own passion and will.

The idea of self-mastery goes back at least as far as Plato, who in the *Phaedrus* described the divided self by using the famous metaphor of the charioteer driving two horses, the black unruly horse symbolizing will, and the white lively one symbolizing passion. The charioteer, signifying reason, must control the horses, must master the irrational will and passion. If either passion or will controls the self, disorder and chaos will ensue. A disordered, unruly self leads inevitably to a disordered, unruly society and government, the great fear of the American Federalists.

Throughout the Middle Ages, as Arthur Lovejoy has shown, educated men conceived the universe as an ordered "great chain of being" whose links ranged in rational and hierarchical order from lowest to highest with difference in kind treated as difference in quality (Lovejoy 59–64). In the eighteenth century, humans were considered the "middle link," halfway between animal and God. The idea of humans as the "middle link," as Lovejoy notes, stresses the duality of human nature as partaking of the divine spirit through the use of reason and of the animal world through the exercise of passion. In Pauline theology humans are both "spirit" and "flesh," torn by conflict and wavering between reasonable thought and action (good) and sensual pleasure (evil) (198–99).

British Enlightenment thinkers argued that the best humans were those who had developed their reasoning faculty. For Locke and other Enlightenment philosophers, reason was absolutely necessary to understand and to create order in an otherwise indecipherable and chaotic world. Only reasonable men could form reasonable societies, and Locke showed Americans that reasonable men could depend on their own judgment (May 10).

In defining American Unitarianism, William Ellery Channing heightened the role of reason in religion by arguing that reason alone should be the guide to interpreting scripture and to leading the Christian life. In "The Moral Argument Against Calvinism," he argues that the "ultimate reliance of a human being is and must be on his own mind. To confide in God, we must first confide in the faculties by which He is apprehended, and by which the proofs of his existence are weighed." Reasoning is our duty because God has given us a moral reasoning faculty whose highest aim is to "form clear and consistent views of God" (Robinson 110). Channing's supposition that people could and should reason about religious matters was anathema to orthodox Calvinists, who, because they considered reason dangerous in matters of faith, kept reason and faith separate. William Ellery Channing based his argument against orthodox Calvinism on this separation.

Associating reason with the ordered hierarchy of Catholicism, John Calvin had discredited the use of reason in religious matters, referring to reason as "Satan's logic." According to Calvin, reason had been corrupted by original sin; thus in explaining salvation, he used the terms "revelation" and "grace." "Revelation" could be experienced first through the senses, but the initial revelatory sense experience must be followed and reinforced by a habitual and personal relationship with God. "Grace," from the Latin *gratia*, was a favor God bestowed on the Elect, those Calvinists predestined for salvation. Calvin's arguments that true Christianity relied on faith, sense experience, and predestination became orthodox Protestant dogma within the Calvinist countries Scotland and America. William Ellery Channing opposed the idea that humans were depraved creatures who could not presume to reason about God. The seeds of his opposition had been planted in Scotland a century earlier.

During the eighteenth-century Scottish Enlightenment, orthodox Calvinism was revised to accommodate Lockean empiricism. The leaders in the revisionist movement were the moral philosophers Frances Hutcheson and Thomas Reid, whose arguments were given a rhetorical turn in the rhetoric texts of George Campbell and Hugh Blair. The Scottish philosophers and rhetoricians, Moderate Calvinists, altered orthodox Calvinist dogma with its Old Testament God of vengeance, its concept of predestination, and its view of human depravity. These revisionists conceived of a benevolent God who, as an example of benevolence, had endowed humans with certain intellective and moral faculties. Merging the Calvinist concepts of "revelation" and "grace" with Lockean psychology, Scottish philosophers argued that with God-given faculties came responsibility to cultivate or improve them. God provided the raw materials that men then should shape and refine through experience and association.

Hutcheson, an early Scottish Lockean who taught moral philosophy at Glasgow, wrote that as the "author of nature," God bestows upon humans faculties, both external such as sight and hearing, and internal such as the power of "perceiving the beauty of regularity, order, harmony" (*Beauty and Virtue* 82). The faculty that forms the core of Hutcheson's moral philosophy is the moral sense, the "determination to be pleased with the contemplation of those affections, actions, or characters of rational agents, which we call virtuous (*Beauty and Virtue* xiv). By allowing men to discern moral conduct, Hutcheson's moral sense operates as a reasoning faculty.

Hutcheson not only conceives a benevolent God but also holds an optimistic view of humanity, a view that contrasts sharply with the Calvinist doctrine of depravity. Nevertheless, for Hutcheson and his followers, depravity was always an underlying theme. Equating depravity with the irrational, Hutcheson says that depravity occurs when reason fails, yielding its control to the emotions since it is "by immoderate ungoverned passions that we are led into vice" (*Moral Philosophy* 64). Hutcheson's fear of "ungoverned passions" echoes Plato's metaphor of the irrational black horse controlling the chariot.

Because men are always in danger of falling under the influence of the irrational, they need to exercise their reasoning faculties, particularly the moral sense, through education. Hutcheson argues, "Those who cultivate and improve this sense find that it can strengthen them to bear the greatest external evils, and voluntarily to forfeit external advantages, adhering to their duty toward their friends, their country, or to the general interest of all" (*Moral Philosophy* 24). In other words, cultivating the moral sense led to the kind of impartiality exercised by the American Founding Fathers. In Hutcheson's view, the most moral individuals are also those who are best educated: "Superior knowledge, we count very honourable; but to mistake, to err, to be ignorant . . . we count evil and shameful" (*Moral Philosophy* 16). Since in Hutcheson's arguments "superior knowledge" is moral and ignorance is evil, then it follows that those people who had access to formal education were the most moral. Hutcheson made explicit what before had been only implicit: that highly educated people, always male, were simply superior in every way to those less educated.

Hutcheson appears to be egalitarian by arguing that God bestows the moral sense to humans at birth. Unlike the Calvinist concept of "grace" which God bestows only to the Elect, the moral sense, according to Hutcheson is "common." Nevertheless, the "common" human mind that receives these gifts is exclusively male. For Thomas Reid, Hutcheson's disciple and the best-known articulator of Scottish Common Sense philosophy, common sense was also moral sense. Reid incorporated much of Hutcheson's moral sense philosophy into his own philosophy, and both he and Hutcheson carefully distinguished between the moral and intellectual capability men are born with and the capability they develop through cultivation and education. God-given faculties, they argued, are only potentialities unless they are developed.

Sometimes the Scottish philosophers used masculinist tropes similar to those of contemporary strength-training. When a faculty was exercised, it grew stronger. Thus conceived, the faculties were like muscles that could be infinitely strengthened by proper use. At other times, however, they used tropes borrowed from horticulture or livestock breeding, with faculties conceived as qualities that needed to be tended, cultivated, and improved. The mixing of tropes indicates a mix of materialism and idealism. If a faculty can be strengthened, then it is corporeal and material. Its need to be cultivated, on the other hand, indicates some ideal notion of perfection toward which a faculty "strives." But the Scottish philosophers were not distracted by metaphorical ambiguity. On the contrary, ambiguity worked in their favor. Instead of using logic as their major persuasive technology, the Scots relied on ethical appeal and the power under Christianity to proclaim. Their rhetorical authority lay not in what they said but instead in who they were. They were ministers first, philosophers second.

Circumventing logical argumentation, Reid bases Common Sense philosophy on "first principles," a term used by Aristotle. Reid's "first principles" are "principles of common sense, common notions, self-evident truths" that are God-given (1:434). It is a first principle, for example, that the "natural faculties, by which we distinguish truth from error, are not fallacious. If any man should demand proof of this, it is impossible to satisfy him" (1:447). First principles embody truths that are basic in areas of logic, taste, and morals. Reid argues that "the virtues, the graces, the muses, have a beauty that is intrinsic. It lies not in the feelings of the spectator, but in the real excellence of the object. If we do not perceive their beauty, it is owing to the defect or to the perversion of our faculties" (1:453). In other words, truth and beauty are real, basic, and irrefutable. If we cannot or do not perceive them, we simply have not developed our faculties properly. The fault lies in human perception and cognition. In Reid's philosophy, therefore, as in Hutcheson's, moral authority is held by those with the most highly cultivated faculties.

Faculties can be cultivated, improved, or strengthened, but they can also become corrupted or depraved by wrong education or bad habits. Then "men may acquire a relish for nastiness, for rudeness, and ill-breeding, and for many other deformities" (1:491). Reid argues that faculties are in danger of becoming corrupted if one associates with the wrong people. Thus, one is judged not only by his own actions but also by the company he keeps. To determine the character of other people, one looks for "signs." Signs of benevolence, Reid maintains, are found in persons of "accomplished good breeding." Good breeding is "made up of looks, gestures, and speeches which are natural signs of benevolence and good affection. He who has got the habit of using these signs with propriety, and without meanness, is a well-bred and polite man" (2:565). One obvious sign of "accomplished good breeding" is eloquent use of words.

The moral philosophy and rhetoric taught at Harvard owed a great deal to the writers of the Scottish Enlightenment, particularly to Hutcheson, Reid, and the rhetorician Hugh Blair, whose text *Lectures on Rhetoric and Belles Lettres,* first published in 1783, was required reading for Harvard students. Blair's *Lectures* was such a popular text that in 1953 Albert Kitzhaber found on Harvard's library shelves twenty-six separate printings issued between 1789 and 1832 (Kitzhaber 50). According to the editors of Edward Channing's *Lectures,* Harvard students read Blair during their sophomore year (xviii). As Douglas Sloan points out, even though Blair was Scottish, his lectures were considered models for Englishmen, even for the critic Samuel Johnson (Sloan 35). Certainly, Blair was required reading for American college men interested in improving their rhetorical styles and in establishing high literary standards. Like the eighteenth-century Scots, the nineteenth-century intelligentsia at Harvard and elsewhere in New England were obsessed with creating and maintaining proper standards for language use, since using proper language was essential for America to establish its high cultural integrity. Though Harvard did not import Scots to teach as did Princeton, the Scottish influence at Harvard was nonetheless potent.

Edward T. Channing's biographer and nephew, Richard Henry Dana, Jr., credits Reid with influencing Channing's rhetorical theory (Dana xvi). Certainly the vocabulary Edward Channing uses derives not only from Reid specifically but also from Scottish Enlightenment philosophy generally. Further, Hutcheson's influence on the thought of William Ellery Channing is well documented. His biographer includes a story about young William reading Hutcheson and experiencing a conversion of sorts. He reported, "I longed to die, and felt as if heaven alone could give room for the exercise of such emotions" (qtd. in Edgell 13). William draws directly from Hutcheson his ideas about a benevolent God who provides humans with a moral reasoning faculty. Both William Channing and Edward Channing, drawing on the philosophy and rhetoric of the Scottish Enlightenment, provide an operational logic and vocabulary—a rhetoric—for an American genteel high culture.

Extending the realm of rhetoric beyond oratory, Edward Channing argues that a "liberal and philosophical rhetoric" should include all forms of composition that aim at "power over the heart." Forms of composition include literature, painting, sculpture, and music—the "elegant arts." If the student wants to practice eloquence in language, therefore, he should visit galleries and symphony halls, since, according to Channing, the compositions there involve the "same principles [as the student's] main pursuit." A broad study of all the arts will enable the student to gain the "completest mastery" of principles and will save him from a "false and dangerous estimate" of his "means of influence" (*Lectures* 33–35).

By placing rhetoric within a community of the "elegant arts," Channing effectively enlarges the role of rhetoric and erases the Aristotelian distinction between rhetoric and poetics. Rhetoric, as Channing envisions it, is "one child of the prolific mother of many arts, which have a common principle or character of perfection" (*Lectures* 34–35). That is, rhetoric like other arts has as its purpose improving human character. Both the poet and the rhetor cultivate their natural faculties. Thus, the poet studies versification and sound until the verse he writes "in its finished state becomes a full exhibition of an inborn faculty" (*Lectures* 48–50). Similarly, rhetoric "takes man with a supposed natural capacity for eloquence, with a language already provided, and the practice of eloquence already existing. Its work is guidance, direction, and further development" of already existing faculties (*Lectures* 42). Rhetorical training therefore should include the "cultivation of acknowledged natural powers and the perfecting of acknowledged natural operations" (*Lectures* 44).

In Edward Channing's *Lectures* "cultivation" mediates the traditional dualism of nature and art. Art is simply nature cultivated. Furthermore, to say that rhetoric's goal is guidance and direction of existing faculties presumes a guide or director, an authority. In the sophistic/Christian rhetorical tradition one cultivates rhetorical faculties by observing those who have already cultivated theirs—orators, writers, preachers, teachers—just as in Unitarian thought one learned morality by observing Christ and following his example. In "Unitarian Christianity" William Ellery Channing argued that though Christ was human, he nevertheless should be regarded as "light, physician, and guide" whose mission was the "recovery of men to virtue" (Robinson 93–94). That Unitarians applied reason to faith did not indicate that they disregarded human experience, especially the communal experience of Christianity. Because the Unitarian concept of reason encompassed common and moral sense, reasoning could not be strictly a solitary activity. Reasonable and moral men naturally followed the examples of other reasonable and moral men.

For William Ellery Channing, Christ was the epitome of reason. Edward T. Channing uses Edmund Burke as an example of a reasoning and reasonable man, who gave a "right direction to public opinion in England on the subject of the French Revolution." Channing describes Burke's accomplishment as follows: "He showed what sorts of innovation were to be dreaded, and what sort of deference to old feelings and old observances was useful and honorable, and what alone it was that deserved the name of freedom. He talked to men who had been in the habit of thinking and feeling correctly; and his triumph of eloquence was in settling the strange disorder of their minds, in clearing the atmosphere of bewildering mists, and saving his countrymen from adopting sentiments of liberty that were as foreign to their whole nature and life as the death-like rule of an eastern despot" (*Lectures* 82).

This passage establishes Burke as moral model, but perhaps more important, it illustrates Channing's version of the liberal consensus. The men Burke addressed had already begun the process of cultivating their faculties. In Channing's words, they were already "in the habit of thinking and feeling correctly," but since Burke's moral and reasoning faculties were more highly developed, he was able to reason more clearly and thus to "clear the atmosphere" and "settle the strange disorder." The men Burke addressed naturally deferred to his superior judgment.

When Edward Channing refers to the "natural capacity for eloquence," he means, as the Scottish philosophers meant, the God-given gifts of reason and language, which were given with the understanding that they should be further developed or cultivated. To the Scottish philosophers, ignorance was a form of evil because it represented a deviation from nature. Good nature (art) was not raw nature, but rather cultivated nature. If one obeys natural law, then one cultivates his faculties. Cultivating one's faculties through study and hard work thus becomes natural, and not cultivating faculties, allowing them to remain in an undeveloped state, becomes, for those who followed the Scottish philosophy, unnatural. The responsibility to cultivate accompanied every gift. Once a man has cultivated his faculties, other men naturally defer to his judgment. Only the highly cultivated carry the authority of eloquence, and men such as Edmund Burke were models for younger men to adulate and emulate. Thus Edward Channing naturalizes cultivation, the authority of the highly cultivated, and the deference the less cultivated owe the highly cultivated.

For Edward Channing faculties were cultivated by studying cultivated men, proper literature, and art. Another means of cultivation was the act of writing, since writing required hard work and diligence. Writing, Channing says, "implies pains and deliberation. The eye being fixed upon the word, a sense of responsibility for the expression is quickened; and more care being required, the power of expression is likely to be better estimated and much enlarged. The eye being fixed upon the written record, a wholeness of view is probably better secured than it would be by sole reliance upon memory, and thus the opportunity and means of correction are always close at hand" (*Lectures* 240).

In Edward Channing's psychology, the goal of writing is control and mastery, the technologies of which are the eye and the hand. As the hand completes the word, the just-written word attracts and captures the gaze of the writer and becomes more than a word—it becomes a sign. The writer who has produced the sign now interprets it. Does it represent his thought? The gaze widens to include more words, sentences, paragraphs. Does this particular word fit with the others? Together, are they accurate expressions of the writer? If so, the word stays; if not, the writer strikes it, corrects it, and moves on.

According to Channing's psychology, writing is a mastering act that carries great benefits, some of which cannot be explained in material terms. The activity itself, Channing observes, seems "to put [the writer's] mind in order and prepare it for manful enterprises which it had shrunk from before" (*Lectures* 241). Channing maintains, "A sincere, strong-minded man . . . is strengthened and animated by the constant succession of ideas distinctly embodied." This strengthening, according to Channing, is the effect of "the mysterious power of a *recorded* word" (his italics, *Lectures* 239).

Edward Channing thus describes the "recorded word" as the product of both responsibility and mastery. But the use of the term "mysterious power" implies some sort of insight where human reason cooperates with divine revelation. William Ellery Channing uses the same psychology and terminology. In "ourselves," he argues, "are the elements of the Divinity" (Robinson 150). Man's higher nature "has its foundation in the original and essential capacities of the mind. In proportion as these are unfolded by right and vigorous exertion, it is extended and brightened" (Robinson 146). For William Channing "right and vigorous exertion" of faculties formed a more moral man, and for Edward Channing, writing was a form of "right and vigorous exertion." The writer's character becomes more cultivated by the act of writing, and writing itself becomes evidence of manliness, mastery, and divinity.

Though neither Edward nor William Channing believed, as orthodox Calvinists believed, that humans are born depraved, they did believe that people can corrupt their faculties by developing bad habits, by neglecting to develop their potential, or by associating with the wrong people. Edward Channing taught, "Many have great deficiencies associated with their native gifts; such as infirmities of temperament and ill-directed or corrupted taste. Instead of instinctively developing the divine faculty, they do all they can to thwart and obstruct it, till at last vicious habits shut it from their sight." Furthermore, there are many cases where "nature has sunk" under instruction by "wrong teaching, negligence, imitation, and tricks and bad habits of all kinds" (*Lectures* 51–55). He taught that "exposure to difficulties" and the "influence of grand thoughts" would enable young men to become less deficient and more perfectly cultivated (*Lectures* 165).

William Channing preached, "It has pleased the All-wise Disposer to encompass us from our birth by difficulty and allurement, to place us in a world where wrong-doing is often gainful, and duty rough and perilous, where many vices opposed the dictates of the inward monitor. . . . We are in the midst of influences, which menace the intellect and heart; and to be free, is to withstand and conquer these" (Robinson 197). Achieving a "free" state involved conquering adverse outward influences by detaching from the world of whirling emotions, by becoming inward and self-controlled. In order to accomplish self-control, one had to follow the "dictates of the inward monitor," the moral reasoning faculty.

For Edward Channing, becoming a cultivated speaker and writer meant putting away the "outward, the material, and the present"—and concentrating instead on the "inward and abstract." Thus, a "mature" speaker or writer does not "make instant proclamation of feelings and ideas," but rather sets a "guard over the tongue" (*Lectures* 52–53). Writers should repress unformed ideas and emotion, Channing argues, because "raw, naked passion" does not "appeal fitly to cultivated minds" (*Lectures*

58). Instead, writers should cultivate the faculty of taste, which Channing describes as that "great moderating or tempering power, that wars against excess, against false associations of images and the unbecoming intrusion of startling but disturbing ideas" (*Lectures* 31). Taste restrains emotions and provides the writer with the "serenity of self-possession" (*Lectures* 59).

The idea of taste as a faculty derives directly from eighteenth-century Scottish philosophy. Hutcheson, Reid, Adam Smith, David Hume, and other less well-known Scottish philosophers had written about the faculty of taste, and Hugh Blair successfully used "taste" as a rhetorical construct. In his *Lectures on Rhetoric and Belles Lettres* Blair posits taste as a "compound power" founded on an internal sense common to all men "in which the light of the understanding always mingles . . . with the feelings of sentiment." Its principles are formed from "consulting our own imagination and heart, and from attending to the feelings of others" (24). Blair argues that exercising the faculty of taste through reading and criticizing literature will improve the "understanding," which will in turn direct the "will" in the "proper pursuit of the good" (13). Thus for Blair, developing taste helps improve one's moral well-being.

Edward Channing embeds in his *Lectures* Blair's concept of taste. Defining taste as an "original faculty or operation of the mind," Channing argues that "its laws or principles [are] as fixed as those of any power, and [it] requires, like any power, a thorough cultivation for a full development." Once cultivated, taste is capable of "never varying truth and excellence" (164). One way of cultivating taste in literature is to read properly. The object of reading is not only "to make one a man of learning and exact taste, but also to form in him that most difficult of all habits, the habit of attention. Then will follow . . . a sharpened power of discrimination, thoroughly disciplined for intellectual work." If students do not read properly, however, they may fall into what Channing calls "literary foppery," which invariably leads to corruption. The moment the student "loses sight of duties and advantages, and begins to trifle miscellaneously with books, and crave variety, and talk of general knowledge . . . there is reason to fear that he is losing all control of himself, and all perception of the useful in reading" (*Lectures* 205).

Channing's language, borrowed from Scottish philosophy and rhetoric, enabled him to associate reading with both morality and utility: reading was a moral act because it was disciplinary and a useful act because it helped cultivate proper taste in reading literature (consumption), and it led to controlled speaking or writing (production). If the speaker or writer has acquired the "taste to discern what manner of speaking becomes the occasion, and if his mind is so balanced that his powers can act together, he has no cause to fear that any faculty will come into action un-seasonably, nor will he meet with a single occasion where it will be nec-essary to suppress his natural temperament." His eloquence, in short, will be "of a high order and influence but unassisted by a single outbreak of passion" (*Lectures* 103–4).

In Channing's rhetorical theory taste, if cultivated properly, becomes a controlling and disciplinary faculty associated with reason. If passion creeps into writing, it must be reasonably justified. That is, it should not be raw passion, but instead reasoned passion. One could argue that in Channing's rhetorical theory reason is little more than calculation and cunning. Channing avoided such charges by linking reason and morality. In America, because of its strong Calvinist/Puritan tradition, morality was always linked with religion, and thus reading and writing properly came to be perceived as moral and religious activities. In this model, lit-eracy, that is, proper and cultivated literacy, is always equated with morality.

Cultivated taste, therefore, refers to much more than high-cultural aes-thetics. In a society in flux, such as American society after the Revolution, taste and cultivation become synonymous and take on special meaning: the condition of public cultivation or public taste becomes a sign of the moral well-being of a whole nation. Thus, in his "Remarks on National Literature," William Ellery Channing calls for a "literature in which ge-nius will pay supreme, if not undivided homage, to truth and virtue; in which the childish admiration of what has been called greatness, will give place to a wise moral judgment, which will breathe reverence for the mind, and elevating thoughts of God" (Robinson 185).

The arbiters of cultivation and taste become articulators and guardians of the moral and cultural standards they set, standards that widen the di-vision between the cultivated and the uncultivated, the civilized and the barbarous. These standards, which define a whole way of life, are endan-gered when the uncultivated masses become vocal and visible. Through-out his *Lectures,* Edward Channing drew sharp distinctions between those who were cultivated and those who were not. While he believed that the elite should try to train the uncultivated to appreciate genteel models of behavior, art, and literature, he held little hope that such training could be accomplished.

Edward Channing praised public lectures, for example, because he thought they had a "civilizing" effect on people who attended. Lectures brought people together, he said, "to have their minds refreshed by truth and their tastes gratified by simple intellectual pleasures." But public lec-tures could never replace formal education. The public lecture, rather, was a "sort of conversation" meant to "stimulate those who are in the habit of thinking and inquiring, to wake up the less intellectual, and to make whole communities feel that they have . . . matters of common interest" (*Lectures* 67–68). In Channing's view, the public lecture was a means of training and elevating the public, by which he meant enabling it to appreciate the standards of the cultivated.

The literary critic served the same function as the public lecturer. Ordinary people sometimes can adequately judge good writing, Channing taught, but they often cannot understand writers of the "highest genius" whose work must be interpreted by "disciples" who "come nearer than [the genius] to the common wants of their kind. . . . [W]e leave the highest criticism in literature in very few hands; not, however, in the hands of monopolists or exclusives, but of the only true radicals,—the men who aim at realizing great ideas." The function of the literary critic/disciple is to translate or interpret the works of the genius for ordinary, less-cultivated people. The critic, more discerning than the common reader, thinks "less of first impressions" and by diligent study becomes aware of the work's "nobler qualities and uses" (*Lectures* 154–60). Reproducing Hutcheson's argument that ignorance is evil, Channing maintains, "[E]vil would fall on writers, and through them on letters, if the great body of readers were really made the arbiters of literary distinction" since writers would be tempted "to write down to their capacity and tastes" (*Lectures* 165). As William Ellery Channing had made clear in his "Remarks on National Literature," American writers should write up instead of down—their purpose is to uplift.

Writing, unlike speaking, has the added advantage of enabling the writers to remain detached from the public they are seeking to elevate. Through practice, the writer learns to master and cultivate objectivity and impartiality, necessary characteristics for the reproduction of a patriarchal system. As I noted earlier, the Founding Fathers were frequently described as possessing God-like impartiality. In his sermon "Likeness to God," William Ellery Channing characterizes the Unitarian God as symbolizing perfect "disinterested benevolence," a concept the eighteenth-century Scottish philosophers created and elaborated in conjunction with "sympathy."

Hutcheson had written that people have a natural "sympathy" or "fellow-feeling" that arises spontaneously and independent of the will. "[T]o be touched deeply with the misfortunes of others," Hutcheson posited, "is honourable" (*Moral Philosophy* 50). The concept of sympathy was for Hutcheson the vehicle for the more abstract concept of benevolence. One practiced benevolence by using sympathy as vehicle. But in Hutcheson's scheme, benevolence must always be disinterested, or checked by reason (*Beauty and Virtue* 140–41).

Among the eighteenth-century Scottish philosophers Adam Smith presented the fullest development of the concepts of sympathy and disinterested benevolence. In *The Theory of Moral Sentiments,* Smith argued that benevolence develops on a societal level from the individual trait "sympathy." Sympathy originates in the imagination when a person places himself in the role of spectator. In this role, Smith argues, we conceive "what we ourselves should feel in the like situation," and are carried "beyond our own person," our impressions copying the feelings of the other person (3–7). For Smith, the concept of sympathy was simple. One simply imagined oneself in the role of observer, and after this imaginative practice became habitual, then one could in a disinterested fashion divide oneself into actor and observer, could become an "impartial spectator."

Smith saw the aim of sympathy as the establishment of a moral society made up of members who had observed the conduct of others and perfected their own conduct to such an extent that they could practice "disinterested benevolence." While sympathy enables one to become benevolent, disinterested benevolence requires reason. The individual remains habitually divided as agent/spectator who is sympathetic/disinterested, passionate/reasonable. In nineteenth-century rhetorical theory, these dichotomies were not described as division but rather as balance and harmony.

In rhetorical theory, sympathy presupposes a certain knowing and a certain shrewd acting upon what one knows. Hugh Blair, for example, posited sympathy as a means of determining the style speakers and writers should adapt according to the ends they want to achieve with audiences. If writers want to please their reading audiences, they should form a "perspicuous" style, a style that pleases because it does not "fatigue" the audience. Blair wrote, "We are pleased with an author, we consider him as deserving praise, who frees us from all fatigue of searching for his meaning; who carries us through his subject without any embarrassment or confusion, whose style flows always like a limpid stream where we can see to the very bottom" (103). By insisting that if used correctly language is transparent, Blair suggests that communication in its highest form eliminates all obstacles to understanding. The highly cultivated writer uses sympathy to develop a transparent style that enables readers to see the world the writer perceives, to see through language.

Edward Channing uses the concept of sympathy to explain how to appeal to readers' common nature. A "writer of the highest genius," Channing taught, has the ability to "go directly to the heart of every man" so that the "reader meets everywhere with something that harmonizes with his usual feelings and experience" and "is agreeably excited without being aware that he is occupied with anything very new, or that requires capacity and resources much beyond his own to produce it." A work may be original and profound yet contain a great deal that is "obvious" (*Lectures* 154–55). Literary works of "unquestionable genius and sincere passion must be marked with a simplicity and obviousness that will make them comprehensible by all" so that "they will be instinctively perceived and felt by the common nature in men" (*Lectures* 153).

Men's common nature, however, enables them only to perceive "unquestionable genius" from a distance. The literary works themselves may be beyond common comprehension; thus, according to Channing, common men's opinions do not "constitute truth." He argues that common men are "pleased with the impulse and guidance that direct them to hidden truth and beauty, and they cannot with so much propriety be said to obey the decree of a master as the decision of their own instructed minds and natural feelings" (*Lectures* 161).

I argued earlier that Channing naturalizes domination by the highly cultivated, and here he naturalizes ordinary people's submission to the "judgments of the more competent." Explaining cultural and intellectual domination and submission in terms of nature reinforces Channing's impartiality—he merely observes and points out the "natural." As Roland Barthes explains the process of naturalization, motives are usually hidden by being cast as reasons (*Mythologies* 129). But in Channing's logic, providing reasons is unnecessary since "reasons" are in the nature of things. By naturalizing cultural domination and submission, Channing has successfully created the myth of a happy, obedient underclass which capitulates to the "natural aristocracy," a disinterested and benevolent group of cultivated speakers and writers. In the process, one could argue, he has managed to secure his own position as teacher of those who want to be masters.

Genteel rhetoric's operative signifier is Edward T. Channing's term the "power of character," a signifier that includes the following traits:

> Mastery as illustrated by education, cultivation of faculties, discipline
> Reason, disinterestedness, impartiality as major governing technologies
> Aesthetics and morality as linked qualities
> Articulation of belief in progress, both individual and national
> Valorization of literary and national patriarchs
> Identification with Boston and New England

Hegemonic practices of genteel rhetoric include the process of naturalization, where domination is described as natural and right. Thus the authority of genteel rhetoric elicits confidence. Because genteel rhetoric's practitioners have access to means of production—higher education, economic advantages, proximity to the publication industry through acquaintance and friendship—genteel rhetoric is prestigious, that is, it becomes legitimized by those it seeks to dominate.

Clarifying Gramsci's concept of hegemony, T. J. Jackson Lears argues that hegemony succeeds not so much by manipulation as by legitimation, that is, when the "ideas, values, and experiences of dominant groups are validated in public discourse" (Lears 573–74). Subordinate groups perceive use-value in the ideas, words, and experiences of the dominant group and act in such a way that they legitimize their domination even though they may at times react against it.

Pierre Bourdieu uses habitus to explain how individuals are inclined to act and react in certain ways. In the editor's introduction to Bourdieu's *Language and Symbolic Power*, John B. Thompson explains that the habitus, acquired through a gradual process of inculcation—childhood experiences and education—"orients actions and inclinations without strictly determining them. It [provides] a 'feel for the game,' a sense of what is appropriate in the circumstances and what is not, a 'practical sense'" (12–13). In the introduction to this study, I argued that cultural capital, those attributes that can be used as signs of prestige, for example Everett's aloofness, are not so much learned as absorbed. Whether one can produce cultural capital is to a great extent circumscribed by one's habitus—what one heard and saw, what one became familiar with, whom one associated with. When Oliver Wendell Homes writes that to become a member of the cultured elite a person must have tumbled about in a library as a child, he is describing this process. The habitus is an inscription upon mind and body.

In writing, the habitus, conceived as those practices and attitudes a writer brings to the rhetorical situation, becomes a major factor when the writer negotiates the constraints of the situation with his or her desire for free expression and self-authorization. To what extent was it possible for Channing's students to resist the imposed authority of genteel rhetoric, to resist reproducing the knowledge and social structures Channing had put into place? To what extent could they invent, create, improvise? In order to consider these questions, I will examine a college essay written by Ralph Waldo Emerson entitled "The Character of Socrates" (*Two Unpublished Essays* 3–39).

Emerson wrote his essay on Socrates in 1820 for the Bowdoin competition, a contest endowed by James Bowdoin, graduate of Harvard, scientist, and governor of Massachusetts. The contest winners received ample cash prizes; in Emerson's day, first prize was fifty dollars, second was thirty dollars. Edward Everett Hale, who first sought publication for Emerson's Bowdoin essays, lists among the 1820 committee of judges

Harvard president John Kirkland and Dr. William Ellery Channing (*Two Unpublished Essays* 4). This committee awarded Emerson second place and did not award a first-place prize, a cruel strategy, I would argue, meant to assert the impeccable standards of the committee and the deficiencies of the writers.

Emerson had often been disappointed during his years at Harvard. Twenty-six years after he graduated in 1821, he wrote his older brother William, "All my life is a sort of College Examination. I shall never graduate" (qtd. in Porte xiii). Emerson found college life oppressive, and he graduated thirtieth in a class of fifty-nine (Allen 58). Van Wyck Brooks describes Emerson's college experience as "four years of a rambling, browsing, fitfully laborious obscurity" (Brooks 27). Though Emerson did not favorably impress his professors and peers, after he became famous, many of them tried to reconstruct their knowledge of him at Harvard. Emerson's classmate Josiah Quincy, for example, wrote, "Of Emerson, I regret to say, there are few notices in my journals." Quincy, however, does mention hearing Emerson read an essay on Socrates, which he describes as a "very good one but rather too long to give much pleasure to the hearers" (qtd. in Holmes, *Ralph Waldo Emerson* 45).

As a third-year student, Emerson did not defy convention nor assume the voice of the prophet of individualism as he did in some of his later essays, such as his 1841 "Self-Reliance." There Emerson wrote that to become self-reliant is to be the "centre of things," the "aboriginal Self." In "Self-Reliance" Emerson writes himself as vigorous, strong-willed, and independent, a freewheeling thinker who negates the influence of his precursors by forgetting what he was "taught in school." Speak your own thought, he says, and don't worry about the consequences. Learn to "detect and watch that gleam of light from within." Don't listen to the "cultivated classes." They are timid, vulnerable, prudent, decorous, feminine. They conform to old usages, they are foolishly consistent, they are mediocre and content (*Selected Prose* 72–93).

As a young college writer, however, Emerson hoped to please the "cultivated classes" enough to bring him the Bowdoin prize. The following long paragraph illustrates Emerson's response to the rhetorical task:

> It will be well, in reviewing the character of Socrates, to mark the age in which he lived, as the moral and political circumstances of the times would probably exert an important and immediate influence on his opinions and character. The dark ages of Greece, from the settlement of the colonies to the Trojan War, had long closed. The young republics had been growing in strength, population, and territory, digesting their constitutions and building up their name and importance. The Persian War, that hard but memorable con-

troversy of rage and spite, conflicting with energetic and disciplined independence, had shed over their land an effulgence of glory which richly deserved
all that applause which after ages have bestowed. It was a stern trial of human
effort, and the Greeks might be pardoned if, in their intercourse with less glo-
rious nations, they carried the record of their long triumph too far to conciliate
national jealousies. The aggrandizement of Greece which followed this memo-
rable war was the zenith of its powers and splendor, and ushered in the decay
and fall of the political fabric.

(*Two Unpublished Essays* 5–6)

In an attempt to impress the judges with his profundity, Emerson grap-
ples with unfamiliar and erudite vocabulary and diction, such as "effulgence of glory" and "aggrandizement of Greece." He also indicates here
his willingness to reproduce language and ideas, for example, the idea
that character is formed by "moral and political circumstances of the
time," and the idea that an "effulgence of glory" may lead to "decay and
fall." Though when he wrote this essay Emerson had not heard Edward
Channing's lectures on rhetoric reserved for seniors, he had read "The Orator and His Times," an address Channing delivered in December 1819 at
his induction as Boylston professor. In preparing to write "The Character
of Socrates," Emerson studied Channing's address, and he borrows Channing's ideas, particularly the distinctions between "ancient" and "modern" orators and the characteristics Channing considered essential for a
moral orator.

In "The Orator and His Times," Channing, imbued with rationalist and
Unitarian notions of progress, compares the ancient and the modern orator. He argues that the ancient orator maintained great power over the ignorant masses, whose minds he formed and whose opinions he regulated.
In turn the orator was shaped by his own imagination and by the flattery
of his audience. Though ancient orators were noble in identifying themselves with national interests, they lacked the "knowledge which makes
men think, and thus lends sobriety to passion" (*Lectures* 4). Channing
characterizes the "spirit" of ancient government as "warlike" and love of
country as cloaking a "boundless ambition of power" (*Lectures* 7). The ancient orator was able to "carry his point by appealing to any principle of
human nature which would aid him, without feeling any responsibility, in
the exercise of his tremendous power" (*Lectures* 9).

In contrast, the modern orator's power is limited by a "more regular
and cultivated" society. Because his auditors are more informed and refined, they are not swayed by passion but rather by the "power of just
sentiments" (*Lectures* 19–20). In sympathetic understanding with his audience, the modern orator becomes "one of the multitude, deliberating

with them upon common interests, which are well understood and valued by all" (*Lectures* 17). Channing's induction speech of 1819 exalts the
power of the moral orator and consensus ideology.

Following Channing, Emerson in his essay characterizes the ancient
Greeks as people of "exalted" taste and "refined" feeling, but "captivated" by the love of "novelty." The Sophists taught the student "forensic
eloquence," which enabled him to "discourse volubly, if ignorantly, on
any subject and on any occasion," they taught him an "imperturbable self-
possession which could confront, unabashed, the rudest accident," and
they taught him a "flood of respondent and exclamatory phrases, skilfully
constructed to meet the emergencies of a difficult conversation." Such
tricks enabled young Sophists to cloak "their sinister designs." Amusing
the "crowds who gathered at the rumor of novelty," Sophists indulged in
"abominable excesses" and thus "degraded the mind" and "debauched
the virtue" of their listeners. "Unhappily for Greece, the contaminating
vices of Asiatic luxury, the sumptuous heritage of Persian War, had but
too naturally seconded the growing depravity" (*Two Unpublished Essays*
8–10). Emerson characterizes Greek audiences as lacking the power of reason, moved solely by caprice or passion. He uses commonplaces that need
neither justification nor explanation: verbs such as "degrade," "debauch,"
and "contaminate" and the noun "depravity," words familiar and un-
questioned in a late Calvinist culture.

Because Emerson wants to reproduce Channing's characterization of
ancient Greeks as too passionate and at the same time to valorize Socrates,
he conceives Socrates as the prototypical Christian hero. He notes that
Socrates first became known as a sculptor but displayed "genius for
higher pursuits," and argues that though he was "educated," the "rudiments of his character and his homely virtues were formed in the work-
shop, secluded from temptation" (11). In opposition to the Sophists,
Socrates has a "sober, dispassionate turn of mind" (14). Emerson thus
tempers the "ancient" Greek temperament with the "modern" ability to
reason, writing Socrates as a reasoning Greek, a "perfect pagan."

He characterizes Socrates as a common man who visited the rich and
poor, the "virtuous" and "degraded," in order to "learn and know mankind" (17) and describes him as teacher whose chief concern was the "care
and improvement of the soul." Emerson positions Socrates as a "distant
forerunner of the Saviour himself" (24–31). Indeed, Emerson's Socrates is
the forerunner of the modern orator Channing describes in "The Orator
and His Times," the orator with religious and civic principles who moves
his audience by the "power of just sentiments."

In "The Character of Socrates" Emerson demonstrates his ability to as-
similate received ideas. His language incorporates and embodies the

dominant ideologies of Harvard and Boston. As writer, Emerson has considered the rhetorical situation and decided to articulate his culture's moral and social values. He has used these values as his own cultural capital. Yet, in the middle of the essay Emerson swerves sharply from the work's ordered course. He changes the subject: "The youth of great men is seldom marked by any peculiarities which arrest observation. Their minds have secret workings; and, though they feel and enjoy the consciousness of genius, they seldom betray prognostics of greatness. Many who were cradled by misfortune and want have reproached the sun as he rose and went down, for amidst the baseness of circumstances their large minds were unsatisfied, unfed; many have bowed lowly to those whose names their own were destined to outlive; many have gone down to their graves in obscurity, for fortune withheld them from eminence, and to beg they were ashamed" (11).

When he writes this paragraph, Emerson's thoughts are not fixed upon ancient Greece or Socrates. Here, he resists reproducing received ideas. Unconnected to what comes before or after, the paragraph stands on the page defiant and self-referential, illustrative of the writer's resistance. Emerson has moved outside the range of appropriate possibilities constructed by cultural expectations and the rhetorical situation. Though he is still using legitimate language, he has changed the topic from Socrates to the sufferings of the "youth of great men," and in doing so, has drawn attention to himself as a writer who is no longer ordered, controlled, masterful, or dispassionate. In the next paragraph, he returns to the topic of Socrates and to his former dispassionate style; yet his resistance manifests itself in other improvisations. He uses "fable" as a verb, as in "to fable forth a being clothed with all the perfection" (4). He describes the morality of the Sophists as "perfumed" (10). He describes Socrates as studying with a "chastised enthusiasm" (14).

Emerson performs as a student writer in the act of authorizing himself as writer. Nevertheless, his writing depends for its authorization on the audience's recognition and reinforcement of his authorial representation. For most of the essay, he improvises within the constraints of the rhetorical situation. He attempts to reproduce what he has learned about Socrates in a discourse that is acceptable, even admirable, to his audience and in a voice that is dispassionate and impartial. He demonstrates respect for Socrates but places him within the context of Christianity by describing him as a precursor of Jesus. He writes in an elevated style, a style already invested with the authority of convention and conformity. Yet he is unable or unwilling to maintain either the style or the topic throughout.

Emerson's essay demonstrates in a concrete way the operation of hegemonic practices. Emerson reproduces the ideas and codes of his culture and of his teacher. He also resists, changes, and twists those ideas and codes. The Bowdoin contest serves as a legitimating practice that reinforces the institutionalization of academic and cultural norms in order to regulate students' writing behavior. In this case authority is situated outside the classroom, with the contest judges assuming the role of pedagogical agents who legitimate the products of culture, institution, and teacher by rewarding the writer who best reproduces those products. The student writer becomes a reward seeker, who, if he desires a prize, must reproduce the intellectual and moral codes of the institution and the culture. He signifies by his reproduction his willingness to become an integrated and submissive member of the dominant culture. This particular Bowdoin contest, whose judges awarded no first prize, served as a legitimating technology of the rhetoric and norms of Boston's genteel high culture.

2

Authorizing High Culture, Authorizing Self

I said to Alcott that I thought the great Man should oc-
cupy the whole space between God and the mob.
                                        —Emerson in his journal

[R]emember that an author's writing desk is something
infinitely higher than a pulpit.
            —James Russell Lowell to Harriet Beecher Stowe

In traditional literary criticism, Ralph Waldo Emerson is usually figured as a major American writer, James Russell Lowell and Oliver Wendell Holmes as minor writers, and Thomas Wentworth Higginson as
noteworthy only as Emily Dickinson's mentor and editor. Yet, all four
writers significantly influenced the direction of letters during the period
called the American Renaissance. They both expressed and demonstrated
their desire to create an American literary high culture with Boston as its
center.

All four writers were instrumental in establishing literary clubs and in
launching the *Atlantic Monthly,* the premier voice of genteel New England
culture, literature, and politics. As key contributors to the *Atlantic,* they established themselves as authorized agents of high literary culture. Models of public intellectuals, these four writer-critics institutionalized a
genteel rhetoric of high culture, remnants of which remain today in cultural and literary criticism. Although the writing of these men differs con-
siderably in style and tone, their vocabulary, themes, and concerns were
strikingly similar. Their lives and their writing were intimately bound
with their Boston environment and with one another. Their success as
writers—their cultural capital—is largely attributable to their habitus,
which included the instruction of Edward T. Channing and the attention

and mentorship of William Ellery Channing. These four writers, as a matter of fact, were bound to the Channing family in several ways.

When young William Ellery Channing became a theology student at Harvard in 1801, he was a member of the church of Dr. Abiel Holmes, father of Oliver Wendell Holmes. Before deciding in 1825 to attend Harvard Divinity School, Emerson studied under the tutelage of William Ellery Channing, who had been an intimate friend of Emerson's father. Together the elder Emerson and Channing created and published the *Boston Anthology,* which William Emerson edited. The *Anthology* was the forerunner of the *North American Review,* for which both Edward T. Channing and James Russell Lowell served as editors. Walter Channing, the younger brother of William and Edward, taught at Harvard Medical School with Holmes. Higginson married Walter's daughter Mary Channing.

This younger generation of writers conceived and wrote William Ellery Channing as prophet. Crediting Channing's philosophy with becoming the foundation of New England Transcendentalism, Emerson describes him as "one of those men who vindicate the power of the American race to produce greatness" (*Selected Prose* 270). At Channing's death in 1842, Lowell wrote a poetic tribute entitled "Elegy on the Death of Dr. Channing":

> From off the starry mountain-peak of song,
> Thy spirit shows me, in the coming time,
> An earth unwithered by the foot of wrong,
> A race revering its own soul sublime.

Lowell creates a Dr. Channing who has shown the way to "Truth" and thus inspired the poet's "hand" to remain "busy" for "Freedom and the Right" (*Poetical Works* 105). These four writers continued to write William Ellery Channing as prophet long after they had finished Edward T. Channing's rhetoric classes at Harvard. While Edward T. Channing helped to form their writing styles and provided the rhetorical theory and vocabulary, William Ellery Channing provided a model for the moral public intellectual and writer.

Born in 1803, Emerson was the oldest of the group of four writers, with Holmes next, then Lowell, then Higginson, younger than Emerson by twenty years. The three younger men grew up in Cambridge. In 1838 when Lowell as a misbehaving student at Harvard was "rusticated" to Concord, Emerson took him for walks and conversation. Emerson, Lowell, and Holmes were sons of ministers: William Emerson at First Church in Boston, Charles Lowell at West Church in Boston, and Abiel Holmes at First Church in Cambridge. Higginson's father served as bursar at Harvard and helped establish the Harvard Divinity School and the American Unitarian Association. Both Emerson and Higginson attended Harvard Divinity School, became Unitarian ministers, and abandoned that career for lecturing and writing.

Besides becoming famous as lecturers and writers, all four men were intimately connected to Harvard. Lowell and Holmes were professors there. Succeeding Longfellow in 1855, Lowell served as Smith Professor of Belles Lettres and Modern Languages for sixteen years. Holmes, a medical doctor, served as Parkman Professor of Anatomy and Physiology in the Harvard Medical School from 1847 to 1882 and as dean from 1847 to 1853. In 1867, Emerson was appointed to Harvard's Board of Overseers and delivered a course of lectures there entitled "The Natural History of Intellect."

Though as an established lecturer and writer Emerson was the central figure in the group, he was not the most publicly visible. The younger three were more active in the world of affairs: Holmes as medical doctor, teacher, and dean; Lowell as editor, professor, and United States minister to Spain and England; and Higginson as minister, abolitionist, and social activist. These four writers not only shared a common interest in and association with Harvard, but they also met regularly in social and literary organizations. Lowell, Emerson, and Higginson belonged to the Town and Country Club. Lowell, Holmes, and Emerson belonged to the Saturday Club. All four belonged to the Atlantic Club whose express purpose was to launch and nurture the *Atlantic Monthly*, which began publication in 1857. Holmes named the magazine, and Lowell said he would accept the editorship if Holmes would be a regular contributor.

These four writers had learned from Edward Channing rhetorical principles that would enable them to perform as highly cultivated writers whose writing demonstrated mastery of knowledge, control of their emotions, and proper moral character. They believed with William Ellery Channing that American literature should manifest the "writings of superior minds." They had watched and listened to Edward Everett as he practiced his "magic of form" and "graces of manner" that Emerson later described. What they had observed and learned became inscribed within their minds and bodies as what David Hume had called "habits of mind," and what the contemporary sociologist Pierre Bourdieu more fully develops as habitus: internalized ways of thinking, acting, talking, and conducting oneself.

Habitus is a process that has the potential to structure or solidify what a person has experienced or learned. As social conditioning, it unifies the practices of those people who have had similar learning experiences in similar familial and social environments. These four writers had similar adolescent experiences, read the same books, studied under the same professors in the same place. Their habitus helped to structure their way of thinking about the world and their conceptions about how they should act, speak, and write. It provided a commonplace, in the sense of *locus communis,* a shared location where they could dwell to escape confusion. For these writers, the habitus also provided the reference material from which they could generate writing that de-scribed their own intellectual and aesthetic experiences and pre-scribed for others. Within their writing, they authorized writing selves that were highly cultured, literate, and moral. By writing for a national magazine, they spread the rhetoric of their genteel New England culture throughout the nation.

To become publicly useful, Bourdieu argues, the habitus is "converted into a disposition that generates meaningful practices and meaning-giving perceptions" (*Distinction* 101, 170–71). As a public resource, habitus is turned to cultural capital. These writers capitalized on their backgrounds and education. They lived at a fortunate time, a time that witnessed the emergence of public writing in newspapers, popular journals, and magazines. The proliferation of public writing occurred simultaneously with the rise of urban capitalism and a new bourgeoisie which read for cultural refinement and self-improvement. Thus the market was exactly right for these new public, high-cultural intellectuals. In *The Market Revolution,* Charles Sellers calls these public writers "a new class of self-making intellectuals" (365). As they created a high literary culture, these public writers created themselves as members of that culture and thus mastered the cultural market.

Lowell, Holmes, and Higginson, in fact, were closely tied by family and social affiliations to Boston's merchant-industrial elite, who funded lecture series. The Boston Brahmins described by Oliver Wendell Holmes in *Elsie Venner* as products of personal wealth, good breeding, and learning began to form a coherent group in the 1790s, when merchant families started to intermarry and forge political and corporate alliances (Hall 181). At that point the Perkinses, Cabots, Quincys, Jacksons, Lawrences, Appletons, Amorys, Lowells, and Higginsons became an integrated group of enterprising elite engaged in overseas trade, banking, building, railroading, and textile manufacturing. As successful entrepreneurs they accumulated wealth, and, true to their Federalist heritage, they balanced commerce and virtue by contributing to Boston institutions. Thus they involved themselves with and contributed money to establishing and maintaining institutions of high culture such as the Boston Athenaeum, the Boston Museum of Fine Arts, and Harvard College.

In 1835, James Russell Lowell's cousin Francis Cabot Lowell established a trust for a series of public lectures on science, history, literature, and the arts to be known as the Lowell Institute. Closely affiliated with Harvard, the Lowell Institute emerged as the nucleus of Boston's intellectual community. James Russell Lowell was invited to deliver a series of lectures there in 1854 and 1855 on "The English Poets." The series was so well received by the Boston cultural establishment that Lowell immediately thereafter was appointed Smith Professor of Belles-Lettres and Modern Languages at Harvard (Heymann 31, 105). Thomas Wentworth Higginson's younger cousin Henry Lee Higginson, a partner in the investment banking firm Lee, Higginson and Company, not only promoted Harvard as a first-rate national institution but also, after the Civil War, used his capital and social resources to found and control the Boston Symphony Orchestra. Years later a writer for *Century Magazine* explained, "The Boston Symphony Orchestra is Mr. Henry L. Higginson's yacht, his racing-stable, his library . . . the place of what these things are to other men of wealth with other tastes" (qtd. in Levine 123). The men promoting high culture in Boston took their responsibilities seriously indeed.

Emerson, Lowell, Holmes, and Higginson were entrepreneurial writers who made their way in the marketplace by selling their ideas and writing. Perceiving and practicing the act of writing as a sacred quest, they authorized themselves as American high cultural specialists. Though they were never as wealthy as other men engaged in business or trade, they were connected to these men through family or social organizations. Further, their lecturing and writing was to some extent supported by the wealthy elite whose money organized and maintained lecture series and magazines. These four writers were practitioners of a genteel rhetoric whose theory and vocabulary derives from Scottish Enlightenment philosophy filtered through and refined by Harvard, Boston, and American Unitarianism. Their writing is genteel because of their culture's association with Christian liberalism, the religion of the head, and their own reading in Romanticism, the secular religion of the heart.

Desiring to invent America by creating and spreading New England's literature and culture, these writers often weighed America against England. Thus, embedded in their arguments about American culture, literature, and character is an anxiety, a fear that democratic America cannot establish a high intellectual and literary culture. As they defy the English literary tradition, they also praise it and are obedient to it. Like Matthew Arnold across the Atlantic, they saw themselves and wrote themselves as apostles of high culture who, in Emerson's words, stood between "God and the mob."

THE IMPERIAL EYE OF EMERSON'S GENIUS/WRITER

In "The American Scholar," Ralph Waldo Emerson introduces genius as the creative principle of "Man Thinking." Books, thoughts, past utterances become inspiration for the "active soul" that *sees* truth and *tells* truth. For Emerson seeing does not mean passively observing as spectator. Rather, seeing provides the agency for individual imagination and creativity. In "Nature," Emerson conceives the eye as the "best of artists," the "best composer" (*Selected Prose* 8). In "The American Scholar" for Man Thinking—the poet, the philosopher—the eye becomes an extension of the mind, a technology of mastery. To see truth, it must penetrate, that is, enter the interior of the Other, and then it loses or diffuses itself in the act of comprehending. Seeing involves penetration/transgression, diffusion, control, cooptation, and gain (Selected Prose 40–55). The "transparent eyeball" of Emerson's "Nature" is "nothing" yet sees all and receives all. The "currents of the Universal Being" constantly and infinitely circulate through it. The "transparent eyeball" apprehends, coopts, and gains (Selected Prose 6).

Emersonian seeing leads to "insight," which Emerson defines in "The Poet" as a "very high sort of seeing" which does not come by study alone, but by the "intellect being where and what it sees" (*Selected Prose* 132). The intellect by means of the eye enters the Other (where it sees), and it becomes the Other (what it sees). The process of seeing and gaining insight does not run outward only but runs inward as well. Seeing is penetration, but gaining insight involves being penetrated, which Emerson describes in "Nature" as an "instantaneous instreaming causing power" (*Selected Prose* 37). Thus when "this feeble human being has penetrated the vast masses of nature with an informing soul, and recognized itself in their harmony," it has "seized their law" (*Selected Prose* 28). The world, then, or the "masses of nature," functions to "make me acquainted with myself." In "The American Scholar" the world becomes the "other me" (*Selected Prose* 45). In "The Poet" Emerson repeats the idea: "The Universe is the externization of the soul" (*Selected Prose* 127).

Now, conceiving the world as other me is different from saying, "I am part of the world" or "I am a world unto myself." Rather than placing the man within the world or separate from the world, Emerson places the world within the man. He continues, "Its attractions are the keys which unlock my thoughts" (*Selected Prose* 45). The world attracts and when the man yields to the attraction, the world becomes a treasure to be appropriated and consumed. In a clever reversal, Emerson figures yielding as an act of conquest and acquisition, or what Mary Louise Pratt calls "anticonquest," where the writer combines "strategies of innocence" with an obvious rhetoric of mastery (Pratt 7).

The model for Emerson's rhetorical turn is Christian conversion, and the master troper is the Jesus of the Sermon on the Mount where the meek inherit the earth and the persecuted are rewarded (see Matthew 5:5,10). When he instructs his disciples, Jesus tells them to be wise as serpents and innocent as doves (Matthew 10:16). In Jesus's teaching, one becomes converted to Christianity or "saved" by becoming dead to the world. In Matthew 10:39, "He who finds his life will lose it, and he who loses his life for my sake will find it." Christian conversion juxtaposes and inverts innocence and wisdom, gain and loss, birth and death, creation and destruction. It is precisely this model of rhetorical inversion that Emerson uses in many of his essays, particularly when he invents the American genius and describes how the genius operates. The American genius, exclusively male, encompasses the scholar, the poet, and the writer.

In "The American Scholar" Man Thinking becomes the "world's eye" and the "world's heart." He "holds by himself" until he "has seen something truly." Then he tells "his brother what he thinks. He then learns that in going down into the secrets of his own mind he has descended into the secrets of all minds. He learns that he who has mastered any law in his private thoughts, is master to that extent of all men whose language he speaks, and of all into whose language his own can be translated" (*Selected Prose* 49). The American genius receives and imparts, knows and promulgates, and, in the process, masters self and audience.

In "Natural History of the Intellect," Emerson reiterates the theme of his early essay "Nature": sympathy and harmony between nature and the human mind. Nature speaks directly to the mind and when the mind "opens" and "comprehends," it "builds the universe and is the key to all it contains" (*Complete Works* 12:4). "Opening" one's mind becomes a process of absorbing and assimilating. Here again is the reversal: yielding becomes controlling and leads to creating. Mind finally is the "creator of the world and is ever creating." Further, the "genius of man is a continuation of the power that made him and that has not done making him" (*Complete Works* 12:15–16). If the world is the "other me" and I/eye have made the world, then I (my mind, my genius) am capable also of creating my self, a self I can infinitely re-create. The vehicle for creating and re-creating is writing. By writing and in writing Emerson builds both his universe and his genius.

Noting that when Emerson was at Harvard he switched to his middle name, Waldo, David Leverenz observes that American Renaissance writers' voices "begin with a self-fashioning beyond yet within the identities given to them by their parents and their culture" (10). Though Leverenz does not mention Bourdieu, his observations about Emerson's re-creations fit within Bourdieu's theoretical concepts of habitus and cultural capital.

Leverenz argues that the emerging middle-class ideology of manhood provided the catalyst for writers' attempts to liberate themselves from British and Puritan/Federalist models. Leverenz perceives Emerson as champion of a newly emerging "manly cultural elite" (61). "The American Scholar" is Emerson's attempt to re-create as manly occupations study, reflection, and writing, to rescue the "study of letters" so that it will no longer be a "name for pity, for doubt, and for sensual indulgence" (*Selected Prose* 55). Thus Emerson managed to turn his personal habits and preferences (his habitus) to cultural capital.

Emerson fashions himself as masculine genius whose eye penetrates the world, and in its penetration, appropriates it. To put Emerson's concept of genius into the rhetoric of Scottish philosophy and Unitarianism, through his eye the American genius observes the world "disinterestedly," finds himself in "sympathy" with it, and appropriates it in order to become a perfect balance of self and world. But Emerson's American genius, a model of taste and balance, neither disrupts nor destabilizes society. In "The Poet," genius "repairs the decay of things" (*Selected Prose* 130). Emerson's genius/writer balances (appropriates) the needs of the world and his own creativity.

Using the language of natural science, Emerson has genius spring mushroomlike from spore, separating from the individual as a "new self," from which detaches a "fearless, sleepless, deathless, progeny" of poems that "ascend and leap and pierce into the deeps of infinite time" (*Selected Prose* 131). These organic metaphors, where things float and fly in search of fertile ground then infinitely divide and multiply, mythicize genius as natural, individual, and male, and the genius's work as spontaneous.

Writing as the work of the genius, an idea propagated by German and British Romantics, was commonplace in Emerson's time. Tracing the evolution of the writer from "*auctor*" to "author" to "genius," Donald Pease notes that the medieval *auctor* commanded authority by organizing accidental events into an established context. Thus, the events in the lives of individuals were subsumed within sacred custom, tradition, or allegory. The author replaced the *auctor* upon Europeans' discovery of the New World, a world that could not be subsumed by reference to cultural, historical, or traditional precedents. In alliance with other "new" men such as explorers, colonists, and adventurers, the author's function was to represent the new, to tell the story of the new to the culture from which he came, to mediate the new and the old. Pease argues that the appearance of the genius/writer signaled the break in the reciprocal relationship between writers and their cultures. Free from cultural determination, the genius/writer, in one sense, stood apart from and above culture, and in another sense, exemplified individual perfection within his culture. Further, the genius/writer's work provided a contrast to other kinds of work: it was "cultural" as opposed to "industrial" (Pease 107–9).

In his inaugural address, Edward T. Channing seemed to be addressing these issues when he said the modern orator, a creature of his circumstances, is but "one of the multitude" whose persuasive power relies on establishing consensus. Where Channing provided a description of what Pease would specify as "author" within a culture, Emerson's genius opposes the conservative tendencies of culture and the drag of his own habitus. The work of the genius—imaginative, organic, and spontaneous— takes on greater significance than the work of ordinary people.

Yet, in "The American Scholar" Emerson calls for an American genius whose ideas are not organic but instead are cultivated. Emerson says that the function of the genius/scholar is the "gradual domestication of the idea of Culture" (*Selected Prose* 51). Within the context of the entire address, the term "domestication" has at least three significations. First, Emerson's program for producing American genius/scholars requires separation from European scholarly traditions, or as Emerson puts it, "We have listened too long to the courtly muses of Europe" (*Selected Prose* 55). In this sense, to "domesticate" is to bring home to America.

Second, Emerson challenges young men to "leave governments to clerks and desks," to abandon public life for a private life of study, reflection, and writing. The private life of such a man, he argues, shall serve as public influence, "shall be a more illustrious monarchy . . . than any kingdom in history" (*Selected Prose* 51). In this sense, "domestication" signifies a retreat from a public life of government or commerce into the self-sufficiency and the "natural" setting of family and home, a setting that enables study and reflection.

Third, Emerson implies that one domesticates the universe by studying the familiar. In the familiar, the American genius/scholar comes to know and control the world: "the world lies no longer a dull miscellany and lumber-room, but has form and order." Where the ideas of the genius/poet operate in an organic universe, the ideas of a genius/scholar create an ordered one. The "shop, the plough, and the ledger" are products of the scholar's domestication (*Selected Prose* 53). The means for discovering the essential order of the universe is the cultivated eye of the genius/scholar, an eye cultivated by studying the detail of familiar and natural things.

Two months before Emerson delivered "The American Scholar" to the Phi Beta Kappa Society in 1837, he published an essay in the *North American Review* entitled "Michael Angelo." In this essay, Emerson praises the artist for studying anatomy. Before he created a statue, Emerson writes, the artist began by drawing a skeleton, then adding muscles, then other dimensions and layers. Michelangelo's study of the form and order of the human body enabled him to lend dignity and authenticity to his art; his "love of beauty is made solid and perfect by his deep understanding of the mechanic arts" (*Complete Works* 12:122). When in "The American Scholar" Emerson remarks, "I embrace the common, I explore and sit at the feet of the familiar, the low," he has in mind studying the form and order of natural commonplaces as Michelangelo studied anatomy. And like Michelangelo the artist, the genius/scholar uses what he learns in the study of nature to create his art. Nevertheless, the "common," the "familiar," the "low" are "embraced" only to the extent that they can be appropriated and used. People, real flesh and blood, are conspicuously absent from Emerson's solitary and utilitarian cultivation of the genius's all-seeing eye. Like the emperor without clothes, Emerson's "transparent eyeball" has no body.

The genius realizes power when he becomes disembodied so that he can convert what he has learned into building materials for his world, his "other me." This conversion is realized in writing. Declaring in "Fate" that "Men are what their mother made them," Emerson attempted in his writing to overcome the body's fate by converting it into public power. "In science we have to consider two things," he writes, "power and circumstance" (*Selected Prose* 218). Circumstance is "what their mothers made"—body, family, race, class, biology, environment, habitus. If circumstance requires a certain compliance, then one turns circumstance to advantage. Fate or circumstance teaches a "fatal courage" that one can use to confront the difficulties of the public world. "For if Fate is so prevailing," Emerson asserts, "man also is part of it, and can confront fate with fate" (*Selected Prose* 222–23). By transforming fate into something he can use—cultural capital—the American genius re-creates himself as master of his own fate while retaining the identity and character (the body or "form and order") imposed on him by family, time, and place. He is born a product of culture, but he becomes a culture producer and a self maker.

If Emerson can turn Fate to useful creativity, he can also turn other Great Men to use, hence the title of the opening essay of *Representative Men*: "The Uses of Great Men." To be of use the great man/genius must inhabit a "higher sphere of thought, into which other men rise with labor and difficulty." Again, the vehicle for entering the "higher sphere" is the eye: great men open their eyes and see things in their "true light" and "large relations," while the rest make "painful corrections and keep a vigilant eye on many sources of error." But Great Men are "related to us" by a universal sympathy that stretches across time, so that "in their character and actions" they answer questions that "we have not yet articulated " (*Works* 2:227–28). James Russell Lowell writes on the same notion in an essay on Shakespeare. While we are trying to read Shakespeare, he writes, we find "he has been beforehand with us" (*Prose Works* 25). In other words, Shakespeare, as genius, has already penetrated/read us. The eye of the genius penetrates and is penetrated, reads and is read.

In "Plato," Emerson brings together the genius/poet and the genius/scholar in the genius/writer. Geniuses "have the shortest biographies," he writes, because they live in their writings. Their "intellectual performance" is what they are (*Selected Prose* 176). We know genius/writers, however, only if we are like them, that is, in sympathy with them. Thus the "mind of Plato is to be apprehended by an original mind in the exercise of its original power" (*Selected Prose* 182). Plato is apprehended as genius/writer not by a disciple but by another genius/writer. Only by writing and in writing does the genius become powerful and vital. He is powerful because he represents and thus controls, domesticates, masters. He is vital by creating a "new self," a disembodied self that is "fearless, sleepless, deathless." In *Manhood and the American Renaissance,* the quotation that shapes David Leverenz's chapter on Emerson is from his 1841 journal: "Give me initiative, spermatic, prophesying man-making words" (qtd. in Leverenz 44). Yet despite his desire for spermatic words, Emerson insists also that the genius/writer be a gentleman.

In his essay "Manners," Emerson distinguishes between mere fashion and gentlemanly manners. Mere fashion, he writes, is "virtue gone to seed." Manners, in contrast, facilitate life and get "rid of impediments" (*Works* 1:320–21). Manners are not necessarily consciously cultivated but are formed from nature and the moral sentiment. They comprise a "graceful self-respect" as well as "deference." Tending to be "intelligent of their merits," gentlemen (men with manners) have a sense of power and get things done easily. They have a "broad sympathy which puts them in fellowship with crowds, and makes their actions popular" (*Works* 1:320). Further, gentlemen tend to associate with each other, establish a "select society," a "self-constituted aristocracy, or fraternity of the best," which perpetuates itself (*Works* 1:316). Oliver Wendell Holmes later elaborates Emerson's idea of a "select society."

The American genius/writer that Emerson desires to create defies convention and at the same time retains it in his manners and in the control of emotions. Emerson believed, as he was taught to believe, that the power to speak and write eloquently, to sway a crowd, is by itself a dangerous talent. Thus, if you arm the man with the "extraordinary weapons of [eloquence], give him a grasp of facts, learning, quick fancy, sarcasm, splendid allusion, interminable illustration,—all these talents, so potent and charming, have an equal power to ensnare and mislead the audience and the orator. His talents are too much for him, his horses run away with him; and people always perceive whether you drive or whether the horses take the bits in their teeth and run." The truly eloquent speaker or writer, always in control, needs "possession" of the subject, a "conviction" that he is right, and a "certain regnant calmness, which, in all the tumult, never utters a premature syllable, but keeps the secret of its means and method." The highest eloquence is founded on strength of character and the moral sentiment. Emerson defines "eloquence" as the "best speech of the best soul" (*Complete Works* 7:90–97).

Emerson's essays reveal his struggle to create a writing "self" that can transcend convention without destroying it. While he writes himself as American genius, he is uneasy with unbridled and unmannered creativity. Despite his preoccupation with individual imagination and creativity, he is nevertheless bound by the rhetoric of Scottish philosophy as it was adapted by American Unitarianism. Thus Emerson's writing is both forceful and gentlemanly, both disinterested and sympathetic. Most important, Emerson believed that those who speak and write should "possess" the quality Edward Channing described as "power of character." The writer should be the "best soul."

Emerson's definition of eloquence as the "best speech of the best soul" echoes Quintilian's definition as the "good man speaking well" and carries also Quintilian's insistence, reinforced by the philosophers and rhetoricians of the Scottish Enlightenment, that the "good man" or "best soul" was the most highly cultivated. Specialists of high culture such as Emerson (and a bit later, Matthew Arnold) use defining terms such as "best soul" self-referentially. By naming and defining the term, the definers create themselves as members of the group. In early national America, those who were permitted to speak and write publicly were men educated in a particular way as members of the elite—gentlemen. Oliver Wendell Holmes makes clear that a man becomes a gentleman by his habitus; that is, a gentleman "should have tumbled about in the library" (*Autocrat* 23). And Emerson argues that one cannot become eloquent with mere "talents" such as "grasp of facts" and "learning." For Emerson, the "best souls" are those men who have become enculturated in the New England tradition and who can convert that tradition into something creative and useful.

Both Lowell and Holmes were members of Emerson's audience for "The American Scholar," delivered before the Phi Beta Kappa Society at Harvard in 1837. In his biography of Emerson, Holmes characterizes the address as "our intellectual Declaration of Independence" (*Ralph Waldo Emerson* 115). Lowell said its delivery "was an event without any former parallel in our literary annals" (qtd. in *Ralph Waldo Emerson* 107). This address and Emerson's speaking and writing in general profoundly influenced the three younger writers, just as Everett's speaking and writing influenced the young Emerson. When they write about Emerson, all three struggle to describe exactly the nature of the influence. Holmes mentions his "epigrammic wisdom," his illustrations as having a kind of "nursery homeliness," and the effect of listening to him as "immediate inspiration" (*Ralph Waldo Emerson* 110–15). Higginson writes about his "pithy and heroic maxims" becoming a "part of the very fibre of manhood" to his generation (*Contemporaries* 14). All three describe Emerson's personal dignity and the mystical element of his influence. Lowell writes, "We look upon him as one of the few men of genius whom our age has produced, and there needs no better proof of it than his masculine faculty of fecundating other minds. Search for his eloquence in his books and you will perchance miss it, but meanwhile you will find that it has kindled all your thoughts." He adds "We do not go to hear what Emerson says so much as to hear Emerson" (*My Study Windows* 376–78).

Emerson provided a model of an American speaker and writer who could utter unconventional statements yet retain an aura of cultivation, dignity, and even conventionality. He could defy the European literary tradition and the Calvinist/Puritan religious tradition in a way that was not radically defiant. He gave younger Harvard-educated men a way to become American writers and remain New England gentlemen, a way to create a high-cultural literary aesthetic that was neither radical nor rude.

LOWELL'S MASTERING METAPHORS

As Smith Professor at Harvard, James Russell Lowell taught courses on the English poets (based on his Lowell Institute lectures), on Dante, and on German, Spanish, and Old French literature, but he made no secret of his preference for English poetry and literature. As the first editor of the *Atlantic Monthly* (1857–1861), he brought his status as Harvard professor, lecturer, and poet to the new magazine, which both he and Emerson envisioned as providing high-cultural leadership (Sedgwick 34). The first issue declared itself "Devoted to Literature, Art, and Politics," designated Boston as its place of origin, and contained an imprint of John Winthrop, Puritan founder of the Massachusetts Bay Colony (Sedgwick 35). As editor, Lowell published Emerson's poems and essays, Higginson's essays, and Holmes's series *The Autocrat of the Breakfast Table* and "The Professor's Story," retitled as the novel *Elsie Venner.* More earnest and high-minded than its chief competitor, *Harper's,* the *Atlantic* appealed to a cultural elite, New Englanders as well as those outside New England. It appealed as well to novice writers such William Dean Howells in Ohio and Emily Dickinson in Amherst.

Lowell considered his duties as professor and his duties as editor to have considerable overlap. That is, his role was, to use Barrett Wendell's term, "interpretive." As professor, instead of strict analysis, he gave students the "spirit" of literature (Wendell 394). He told them how literature serves cultivation. As literary and cultural critic, Lowell smarted under the attacks of English critics such as Sydney Smith who in the *Edinburgh Review* had asked, "Who reads an American book?" (qtd. in Lowell, "Nationality" 200). The implied answer is that nobody reads an American book since Americans do not have enough sense of history and art to write books. In "Nationality in Literature," Lowell redefines the debate by arguing that no great literature is strictly national: "The key by which we unlock the great galleries of Art is their common human interest ("Nationality" 201). America, he argues, rather than being without a literature, is heir to all great literature including that of England: "As if Shakespeare, sprung from the race and the class which colonized New England, had not been also ours!" ("Nationality" 202).

This nation, he stipulates, never had a "proper youth," a "mythic period," from which writers can draw material for literature or poetry: "They cannot, as did Goethe in his Faust, imbue an old legend, which already has a hold upon the fancy and early associations of their countrymen, with a modern and philosophical meaning which shall make it interesting to their mature understandings and cultivated imaginations" ("Nationality" 204). This argument, stated by many English critics and repeated by various American intellectuals from Edward Everett through Henry James, presents the essence of the problem for American writers: they have no mythic past. This problem assumes that great literature, depending upon a rich intellectual and cultural heritage, is the product of highly cultivated minds able to draw on accumulated historical experience.

Lowell fails to acknowledge that the American Eden was populated with people who did have myths. The reproduction of the myth of the absence of myth provides a striking example of the colonial mentality which successfully obliterates native myths and legends by refusing to consider them as proper literary material. To do so would be to admit the humanity of the people considered primitive, barbarous, and uncultivated. In Lowell's definition literature is, as William Ellery Channing defined it, "the writing of superior minds," but "superior minds" come from the European tradition. Lowell thus finds himself in a bit of a bind, a bind from which he can escape only if he claims English literature as his own. Thus Lowell abandons the topic of American literature by arguing that this country's genius lies in developing and "practicalizing simpler and more perfect forms of social organization." If he cannot beat the English at the literary game, well then, he can change the subject. He continues: "We

have yet many problems of this kind to work out, and a continent to subdue with the plough and the railroad, before we are at leisure for aesthetics. Our spirit of adventure will take first a material and practical
direction, but will gradually be forced to seek outlet and scope in unoc-
cupied territories of the intellect. In the meantime we may fairly demand
of our literature that it should be national to the extent of being as free
from outworn conventionalities, and as thoroughly impregnated with humane and manly sentiment, as is the idea on which our political fabric
rests" ("Nationality" 209).

Instead of defending American literature against the attacks of English
critics, Lowell argues that the idea that great literature belongs to a particular nation is false. If a literature is "national," then it is provincial and
narrow, a "sublimer form of clownishness and ill-manners" ("Nationality" 208). Furthermore, he argues, Americans are too busy with material
and practical matters, having, after all, a "continent to subdue with the
plough and the railroad," metaphors I will comment upon momentarily.

For now, I want to emphasize Lowell's rhetorical strategy of equating
"national literature" with provincialism and rusticity, a move that effectively turns the argument of the English critics. Lowell stipulates that
America has no mythic past, but argues further that Americans, that is,
Anglo-Americans, can draw on the mythic past and cumulative history of
Europe. Literature, his argument goes, should not be the product of a single nation. In an essay on Chaucer, Lowell writes that "Poets have forgotten that the first lesson of literature, no less than of life, is the learning how
to burn your own smoke; that the way to be original is to be healthy; that
the fresh color, so delightful in all good writing, is won by escaping from
the fixed air of self into the brisk atmosphere of universal sentiments; and
that to make the common marvelous, as if it were a revelation, is the test
of genius" (*My Study Windows* 228).

Here Lowell creates the good chimney as a metaphor for the genius-
writer. If a chimney proves incapable of burning its own smoke, then the
air becomes, in Lowell's words, "fixed," that is, motionless and stifling.
While subject matter for American writers may be regional or national,
that is, circumscribed by place like the chimney, the themes should be
common ones so that they can escape into "universal" air. Great literature,
Lowell argues, rather than belonging to a particular nationality, belongs
to and addresses universal human nature.

As the chimney receives heat, the writer receives inspiration and produces good writing that rises like smoke until it enters the realm of the
universal or divine. Of Dryden, Lowell writes that his mind warmed
slowly, but once heated, "he had more of that good-luck of self-oblivion

than most men" (*Prose Works* 143). Dryden "sometimes carried common sense to a height where it catches the light of a diviner air" (*Prose Works* 187). In this instance, the attention shifts from the good chimney to the smoke—the writing. An accomplished writer, like a good chimney, produces writing that does not call attention to the writer. Rather, as Hugh Blair advocated, clear writing produces reality. Because of the transparency of carefully chosen words, the reader sees through the words to reality, and in the process, the writer becomes obliterated. His reality is not merely *his* reality but common and universal reality. Like a good chimney, the writer performs without calling attention to himself. According to Lowell, a self-conscious writer is but a "second-class genius" who can be detected by his "mannerism, for that, being an artificial thing, is capable of reproduction" (*Prose Works* 38). A first-class genius produces not the artificial but the real.

Because, in his view, the production of the real depends on the character of the writer, Lowell's erasure of the author is unsuccessful. But when Lowell argues that writing should not self-consciously call attention to the writer, he was proscribing only a certain kind of self-conscious style, the style of a writer who is inexperienced, imitative, or too correct. Lowell's own writing certainly called attention to Lowell by its erudition, its obscure words, its didactic tone. Furthermore, even though while he was editor essays published in the *Atlantic* were unsigned, people who knew the writers could guess who the authors were by the essays' style and content.

Like the other writers whose works he published, Lowell was erudite, but in the introduction to the second series of *The Biglow Papers* he argues that American writing should be both simple and masculine. He uses Abraham Lincoln as his model, characterizing him as "master . . . of a truly masculine English, classic because it was of no special period, and level at once to the highest and lowest of his countrymen" (*Biglow Papers* ix). Lowell fears that American writers tend to be too conventional:

That we should all be made to talk like books is the danger with which we are threatened by the Universal Schoolmaster, who does his best to enslave the minds and memories of his victims to what he esteems the best models of English composition, that is to say, to the writers whose style is faultily correct and has no blood-warmth in it. No language after it has faded into *diction,* none that cannot suck up the feeding juices secreted for it in the rich mother-earth of common folk, can bring forth a sound and lusty book. True vigor and heartiness of phrase do not pass from page to page, but from man to man, where the brain is kindled and the lips suppled by downright living interests and by passion in its very throe. . . . There is death in the dictionary; and, where language is too strictly limited by convention, the ground for expression to grow in is limited also; and we get a *potted* literature, Chinese dwarfs instead of healthy trees.

(*Biglow Papers* xi)

Here Lowell's prose, his metaphors for masculine creation, become, as Emerson's often are, homoerotic, describing American writing as male vitality, desire, or interpenetration. His writing here is reminiscent of Whitman, who later uses similar terms to figure a radical democracy where political and sexual identity would be fused (Newfield 92). But Lowell's call for a "blood-warmth" masculine style is not democratic like Whitman's. Writers, he insists, are formed like trees from the soil out of which they grow. They are cultivated. They are not "sudden prodigies, but slow results," drawing their force "out of the decay of a long succession" of writers who have gone before. In proportion as the "genius is vigorous and original will its indebtedness be greater, will its roots strike deeper into the past and grope in remoter fields for the virtue that must sustain it" (*My Study Windows* 234). To become cultivated means that the writer must look backward to past writers for wisdom and inspiration as well as forward to "remoter fields," other territories perhaps as yet unmapped.

In "Nationality in Literature" Lowell refers to the plough and the railroad as instruments for subduing the continent, a reference that indicates the connection between cultivation and conquest. If "remoter fields" are the source of virtue, then they should be found, mapped, conquered, and cultivated. To cultivate the land meant that the farmer or gardener uses the power of nature for human good. By the middle of the nineteenth century, Americans had effectively rationalized that harnessing natural resources in no way harmed nature, but instead actually fulfilled nature's purpose (Kasson, *Civilizing* 3). Cultivating nature was naturally good. For Edward Channing, cultivated nature is art. Emerson's nature, inspirational and spiritual, is also a resource, a commodity. Lowell's plough and railroad, examples of technological innovation essential to progress, were linked to commodification and marketability. To "subdue a continent" meant to cultivate it, to make it worth something, to convert it to capital.

One of the many societies that the New England male elite created was the Massachusetts Society for Promoting Agriculture, formed in 1792. Many of its members owned country estates where, as gentlemen farmers, they gardened and experimented in agricultural research, pastimes they considered appropriate and even moral for men of their station. The MSPA collaborated with Harvard to establish a professorship of natural history and to maintain a botanical gardens at the college (Thornton 63–64). Thus at Harvard cultivating soil and cultivating minds became institutionalized as part of the same cultural aesthetic. Distinguishing the flowers from the weeds was the same as distinguishing the civilized from the savage. Flowers and the civilized were products of cultivation, and if weeds and savages could not be domesticated by cultivation, well then, dispose of them.

The plough and the railroad, interesting as they were as symbols of cultivated progress in New England, held greater promise as instruments of western expansion. The train in particular captured the imagination of the apostles of American progress. With its speed, efficiency, and regularity, the railroad represents the triumph of rationalism. By 1840, while Europe had only 1800 miles of railroads, this country had 3000 miles with over 2000 miles in the New England and Mid-Atlantic states. By 1860, the railroad track became a national network covering 30,000 miles (Foner and Garraty 906). Though Lowell sometimes conveniently used the railroad as a metaphor for progress, he also understood its potential for democratization.

In 1884 he delivered an address in England on American democracy and again used the train as metaphor, but this time in a different way: "Some people advise us to put on the brakes, as if the movement of which we are conscious were that of a railway train running down an incline" (*Democracy* 16). Lowell uses the runaway train as metaphor for the runaway tendencies of democracy, the anarchy that might result when the masses take charge. Yet Lowell also argues, "[T]he question is no longer the academic one, 'Is it wise to give every man the ballot?' but rather the practical one, 'Is it prudent to deprive whole classes of it any longer?'" (*Democracy* 31). As an older man Lowell turns away from not only the radical ideas of his youth but also from the notion of progress in general. Where the vote is concerned, prudence takes the place of progress. Whereas in antebellum America civic virtue and the ballot had been the privilege of the propertied white male, Lowell argues in 1884 that everyone (all men?) should be allowed to vote. But though the masses should have a voice in political matters, Lowell is unwilling to concede that they are cultivated: "Let me not be misunderstood. I see as clearly as any man possibly can, and rate as highly, the value of wealth, and of hereditary wealth, as the security of refinement, the feeder of all those arts that ennoble and beautify life, and as making a country worth living in. . . . Old gold has a civilizing virtue which new gold must grow old to be capable of secreting" (*Democracy* 29).

Lowell seems to be arguing that the power of the vote is very little power at all. The real power, the "civilizing virtue," is the power of the monied aristocracy. Given Lowell's arguments, to title his address "Democracy" is ironic, to say the least. Lowell's rhetoric, fragmented and incoherent, exemplifies the problems of a writer who attempts to write about America as if it were one unitary culture. Emerson at least admitted his inconsistency; Lowell tried to portray America as democratic while his rhetoric became increasingly elitist.

THE SNAKE AT THE BREAKFAST TABLE

Before Oliver Wendell Holmes began to build his wider reputation as a writer by publishing in the *Atlantic,* he was famous in Boston circles as a conversationalist whose genial nature allowed him the privilege of making outrageous statements. Thomas Wentworth Higginson, for example, tells the story of a particular Atlantic Club dinner given in the honor of Harriet Beecher Stowe, who had accepted the invitation on the condition that no liquor would be served. Higginson reports that the sober dinner curtailed the usual lively conversation and that Holmes spent the evening trying to convince Stowe's husband, Calvin Stowe, an orthodox Calvinist minister, that "swearing doubtless originated in the free use made by the pulpit of sacred words and phrases" (*Cheerful Yesterdays* 179). Holmes, who was always highly entertaining at these functions, believed that Calvinism deterred rational human progress, and in much of his writing he satirized Calvinism. In one of his famous poems, "The Deacon's Masterpiece," the deacon builds a wonderful one-horse shay (Calvinism) that finally disintegrates, "just as bubbles do when they burst." The poem ends "Logic is logic. That's all I say" (Cook 70). For Holmes as for William Ellery Channing, logic and reason naturally reject strict Calvinist dogma.

Holmes's novel *Elsie Venner* was originally published serially in the *Atlantic Monthly,* beginning in December 1859 under the title "The Professor's Story." Holmes calls *Elsie Venner* a "medicated" novel, though it is better described as early science-fiction. Holmes clearly exploits the novel genre for his rhetorical aims, and at times loses sight of plot and characterization in order to make his points. The novel is peppered with digressions, outright arguments, Yankee dialects, and a black vernacular dialect, as well as characterizations of New England country folk, a mixed-blood foreigner, and a black woman. While Holmes says he "aims to test the doctrine of original sin and human responsibility" (ix), he does not really explore or test these ideas but rather puts forth the argument that what happened to Elsie in utero structured her mental and moral faculties.

The central character is eighteen-year-old Elsie Venner, who is afflicted with "ophidian tastes and tendencies" as a result of her mother's being bitten by a rattlesnake before Elsie's birth (xii). The mother dies, and Elsie is raised by her father and by Sophy, her housekeeper and confidante. The setting of the story is Rockland, a country town on the margins of civilization, whose principle feature is The Mountain (Holmes's capitalization), which Holmes describes as "beautiful, wild, invested with the mystery which belongs to untrodden spaces, and with enough terror to give it dignity" (53). Not only does The Mountain have a rocky precipice that hangs over the village as a constant threat, but it also has a region called Rattlesnake Ledge, "tenanted by those damnable reptiles" that, despite several attempts, the townsfolk cannot eradicate (43). Elsie, who has snakelike features, often runs away and hides on Rattlesnake Ledge, and, though she attends the local school for girls, she has no friends because her appearance and behavior frighten people. As the family doctor tells the schoolmaster Bernard Langdon, "Her love is not to be desired, and . . . her hate is to be dreaded" (212). Langdon confides to the doctor that "there must be something in that creature's blood which has killed the humanity in her" (214).

Langdon's concern leads him to inquire about Elsie's behavior in a letter to his former professor of medicine (Holmes's occupation), who answers that it is possible that prebirth events could limit the "sphere of the will" (225). According to the authoritative professor, people err by equating crime with sin. Moral defects should be considered the same as physical and intellectual defects; that is, people may be morally defective through no fault of their own and therefore should not be blamed or punished (226–27). Thus about halfway through the novel, Holmes has the authoritative professor settle the central issue. But Holmes keeps writing. The major issue having been dispensed with, the latter half of the novel is not about how far human responsibility extends; rather, it becomes Holmes's commentary on class and race.

Holmes divides the houses of Rockland into three categories: the luxurious mansion house with dormer windows, a balustrade, and a "good breadth of front-yard"; the less grand genteel house, two-story but "cheerless and unsatisfactory"; and the unpretentious farmhouse, which has a "good warm kitchen" where one can be comfortable "without fear and without reproach" (57–59). Holmes uses houses as metonyms to describe the people who inhabit them. The inhabitants of both the mansion and the farmhouse are authentic, though one group is authentically rich and the other authentically poor, but the inhabitants of the "genteel" house pose and pretend.

The Sprowles's genteel house has "some pretensions to architectural display" that make it appear a little "swaggering" to Bernard Langdon, to whom the house "implied a defective sense of the fitness of things" (81). Holmes describes in detail a party at the Sprowles's to make his point that a party given by the "smaller gentry" is a solemn rather than a celebratory occasion (87).

In contrast to the pretentious Sprowles, the Venners—Dudley and his daughter Elsie—live on a large estate in a mansion house "fat with the deposits of rich generations which had gone before." Elsie possesses "precious old laces," a closet full of silver, and books in the library "ordered from the great London houses, whose imprint they bore, by persons who knew what was best and meant to have it" (197–98).

Even though the Venners are wealthy, that they live in rural Rockland precludes them from membership in the "Brahmin caste of New England." This is the caste of Bernard Langdon, the gentleman-schoolmaster, a former medical student who, because his family has fallen on hard times, quit his studies and took a teaching position. The Brahmin caste is the "harmless, inoffensive, untitled aristocracy" that comprises "races of scholars . . . in which aptitude for learning is congenital and hereditary" (4). As the only gentleman-scholar and the sole member of the Brahmin caste in Rockland, Langdon is clearly out of his natural environment, and, in the end, he returns to the city.

Rather than basing class distinctions on wealth, Holmes categorizes each class on the basis of certain essential features. The Brahmin caste, the "untitled aristocracy," has certain aptitudes that are inbred and inherited. One is a Brahmin by being born into a Brahmin family, whose taste and learning has been cultivated for generations. To try to move up the social ladder in a generation, as Langdon notes when observing the Sprowles's house, implies "a defective sense." Things are out of kilter; they do not fit.

In *The Autocrat of the Breakfast Table*, Holmes elaborates on this theme by comparing a "self-made man" to that "Irishman's house on the marsh at Cambridgeport, which house he built from drain to chimney-top with his own hands." Though it was a "good house for a 'self-made' carpenter's house," it was a "little out of plumb, and little wavy in outline, and a little queer and uncertain in general aspect." Just as he was incapable of building an unblemished house, the Irishman who tried to participate in self-making was bound to fail. He was not a "man of family," that is, a "man who inherits family traditions and the cumulative humanities of at least four or five generations. Above all things, as a child, he should have tumbled about in a library. All men are afraid of books who have not handled them from infancy" (19–23). Self-made people, Holmes suggests, may acquire all the accouterments of high culture such as wealth, knowledge, and refined taste, but they can never be Brahmins. No matter what they accomplish, they remain "afraid of books." So goes Holmes's comment on class.

The three most intriguing characters in *Elsie Venner* are Elsie, her cousin Dick Venner, and her housekeeper/confidante/maid Sophy. Holmes uses these characters to comment on race. Because she was infected with snake venom in the womb, there are "two warring principles" within Elsie, "contradictions in her moral nature,—the longing for sympathy . . . and the impossibility of passing beyond the cold circle of isolation within which she had lived so long" (434). As her doctor says, "She has lived a double being" (445). In the end, Elsie begins to look like her mother and longs to be loved. When she becomes overwhelmed with a "sudden overflow of feeling which broke through all the barriers," Elsie weeps and thus drives away the "evil spirit" which had pervaded her being (442). Then, of course, she dies.

Elsie's cousin Dick Venner is the son of Dudley's brother, a South American trader, and a "lady of Buenos Ayres, of Spanish descent," who had died when the boy was an infant. The willful Dick had attended school in "Buenos Ayres," quarreled with relatives, and accompanied Gauchos and Indians on "some of their savage forays" (154). Now back in New England, he is determined to woo Elsie and inherit his Uncle Dudley's fortune. Convinced that the Brahmin schoolmaster is in love with Elsie, Dick tries to eliminate his competition by lassoing and hanging him. The plan fails when Langdon is rescued by a townsman who has suspected the "Portugee" of foul play. Dick is described at various times as "half Injin," as "dangerous looking," and as having hot-blooded "Southern impulses."

Holmes writes that "Dick had two sides in his nature, almost as distinct as we sometimes observe in those persons who are the subjects of the condition known as *double consciousness*. On his New England side he was cunning and calculating, always cautious." But at times he had "fits of jealousy and rage," which could transform themselves into dangerous forces if they combined with his New England "cool craftiness" (356).

Sophy is introduced to the reader about halfway through the novel as the old black housekeeper who has taken care of Elsie since she was a baby and as the only human Elsie can love (179). Sophy's "keen, concentrated watchfulness" and instincts enable her to gain insight into Elsie's personality, and in fact, she is the only person who understands Elsie and can discern her moods (260). Like Elsie and Dick, Sophy's nature has two sides. Holmes writes that her grandfather, a cannibal chief, "was in the habit of inviting his friends to dine with him upon the last enemy he had bagged, and that her grandmother's teeth were filed down to points, so that they were as sharp as a shark's" (348). Yet despite her heritage, Sophy has developed a Christian love for Elsie, so much so, that when Elsie dies, Sophy dies soon after and is buried at the foot of Elsie's grave. Holmes writes, "If there were tears shed for her, they could not be bitter ones; for she had lived out her full measure of days, and gone—who could help fondly believing it?—to rejoin her beloved mistress. They made a place for her at the foot of the two mounds. It was thus she would have chosen to sleep, and not to have wronged her humble devotion in life by asking to live at the side of those whom she had served so long and faithfully" (466).

Even though Elsie and Dick are irredeemable, neither is a tragic nor even a serious figure. Rather, the novelist uses these figures to signify "doubleness." Sophy alone, though she dies of grief, is redeemed by her "humble devotion," which compels the author to have her buried at the foot of Elsie's grave, her proper place—the place that she, of course, would have wanted. Though Holmes has created an obedient and devoted Sophy, he has also created a Sophy with humane characteristics; therefore, it could be argued that Sophy personifies the writer's liberal tendencies, liberal as measured by nineteenth-century standards. Yet Sophy, too, suffers what Holmes calls a "double consciousness." The double consciousness of each of these three characters is "caused" by biological conditions: Elsie is half human and half snake, Dick is half Anglo-American from New England and half "Portugee" from Brazil, and Sophy has inherited the barbarism of her African grandparents but has adopted the Christianity of New England. With Elsie and Dick, the "doubleness" leads to duplicitous personalities, whereas Sophy's "doubleness" leads to death, which to Holmes seems the better fate.

In contrast to the three characters with double consciousness, Bernard Langdon is a "perfectly gentlemanly young man" who means what he says. The narrator comments, "When you find a person a little better than his word, a little more liberal than his promise, a little more borne out in his statement by his facts, a little larger in deed than in speech, you recognize a kind of eloquence in that person's utterance not laid down in Blair or Campbell" (9).

In Bernard Langdon, Holmes has created a character who is balanced and whole, who has what Edward T. Channing called "power of character." Langdon is as confident of his place in the world as Sophy is of her place, though the two places are hardly similar. Where Sophy requires Christian devotion to redeem her from "doubleness," Langdon needs no such redemption since, as a Brahmin, he is incapable of ignoble thought or action. Like Channing's grandfather William Ellery, Langdon had an "invisible virtue" powerful enough to make him exceptional.

Half a century after the publication of *Elsie Venner,* W. E. B. Du Bois describes the concept of double consciousness in sociological terms. In *The Souls of Black Folk,* Du Bois does not write from the privileged position Holmes occupies but rather from the position of one born into a "world which yields him no true self-consciousness, but only lets him see himself through the revelation of the other world." Du Bois describes double consciousness as a "sense of always looking at one's self through the eyes of others, of measuring one's soul by the tape of a world that looks on in amused contempt and pity" (8). For Du Bois, the African-American longs to "attain self-conscious manhood, to merge his double self into a better and truer self" (9). The characteristic Channing describes as "invisible virtue," Holmes as an "eloquence" not found in Blair and Campbell, and Du Bois as a "better and truer self," is the unified self, that is, a single, co-herent self balanced perfectly between thought and action, between virtue and truth. For Holmes and other genteel writers, male Brahmins could as-sume as natural the unified self for which Du Bois longed. That the uni-fied self was a myth apparently never entered these writers' minds.

Boston's intellectuals, perfectly unified selves, needed others like themselves for congenial company. In *The Autocrat of the Breakfast Table*, Holmes describes a "Society of Mutual Admiration . . . a social develop-ment which belongs to the very noblest stage of civilization." He writes that men of genius, or any other kind of superiority, admire the same qualities in others, and therefore, all artists, authors, and scientists ought to form Societies of Mutual Admiration. Such societies are hated and feared by foolish people, Holmes writes, because they are lofty, serene, impregnable, and of necessity, exclusive (2–5).

As Holmes was writing and publishing *The Autocrat* serially in the *At-lantic* in 1857, the Saturday Club was being formed with Emerson as founding father (Duberman 184). Several years earlier, Emerson also had been instrumental in forming the Town and Country Club, whose mem-bership included Emerson, Holmes, Lowell, and Higginson. In 1849 Low-ell and Higginson decided to propose the membership of Frederick Douglass, but opposition developed to Douglass's membership, and in a letter of 23 July 1849 Lowell wrote to Higginson that he was "astonished at the quarter from which it came." Lowell believed that if the matter had been put to a vote, "Emerson would have blackballed Douglass" (qtd. in Wortham 297). Douglass's membership was never proposed. Because the Town and Country Club had become too big and unwieldy, the Saturday Club was formed as smaller and more exclusive.

The Saturday Club's first members included Emerson, Louis Agassiz, Benjamin Peirce, and Richard Henry Dana, Jr. James Russell Lowell was invited soon thereafter. Oliver Wendell Holmes, however, had not yet been asked to join when he described the Society of Mutual Admiration in *The Autocrat* series. His description was an obvious reminder that he had been overlooked, and he was immediately invited to join the exclu-sive club. Higginson, however, never was invited to join since most mem-bers considered his abolitionist views too radical.

The subtitle of Holmes's *The Autocrat of the Breakfast Table* is "Every man his own Boswell." Holmes characterizes Boswell as "most admiring among all admirers" (4). By choosing this subtitle, Holmes plays on two divergent themes. The phrase substitutes "Boswell" for "priest," in the well-known Calvinist slogan "Every man his own priest." This slogan signifies to Calvinists that the priest has been removed as mediator between humans and God. People could read the Bible, interpret scripture, and pray directly to God without the intervention of the priest. In this sense, men, at least—Calvinists would never consider the possibility of women as priests—confronting God and religion unassisted, are raised to the level of the priesthood.

Second, Holmes's audience would recognize James Boswell as Samuel Johnson's biographer who held such fawning admiration for Johnson that he was unable to write about him except to praise him. If every man were his own Boswell, then he would be his own most ardent admirer. Both meanings come into play in the persona of the autocrat. As the domineering figure at the boarding house breakfast table, the autocrat is both priest and his own admirer.

Writing in the persona of the autocrat, whose personality is very similar to his own, allows Holmes to reveal aspects of himself that would otherwise be inappropriate. He reveals, for example, the fault of talking too much, of not listening when other people talk, of having strong opinions that he voices mercilessly even when his audience no longer pays attention. His brand of humor, therefore, is a kind of self-mockery that is good-natured and clever enough to have a disarming effect on readers.

For instance, the autocrat wonders why authors try not to be funny and decides that there must be deep philosophical reasons. "Passion never laughs," he concludes. "The clown knows very well that the women are not in love with him, but with Hamlet, the fellow in the black cloak and plumed hat. . . . The wit knows that his place is at the tail of a procession." The autocrat then defines the essence of wit as casting an "incomplete view of whatever it touches." It throws a "single ray, separated from the rest" but never "white light; that is the province of wisdom" (50).

At times Holmes writes the autocrat as fool, but just as he may begin to appear too foolish, Holmes changes the tone of the discussion by moving from self-mockery to seriousness. The seriousness and intelligence of the analysis of wit undercuts the self-mockery, and just as it does, Holmes again changes the tone. As the autocrat asks if they will allow him time to pursue the subject further, a chair scrapes the floor, and everyone but the autocrat leaves the table. The writer/narrator mocks himself for talking so long that his audience abandons him.

Holmes's kind of congenial self-deprecation can be written only from a position of high social status and self-confidence. Writers with less social status or less confidence cannot make this kind of play operate to their advantage, nor are they likely to try. Self-mockery, after all, invites others to look at the writer's deficiencies, something less confident writers can ill afford. Self-mockery has a disarming effect only to the extent that the audience wishes to identify with the writer/narrator. In that case, readers are willing to look at the deficiencies, identify with them, and then overlook them. If the writer can diffuse negative responses, then he or she succeeds in exercising a certain amount of control over his or her audience.

Holmes carefully controlled his public persona and his readers' reactions. Until the Civil War, the topics of Holmes's essays—unlike those of Emerson, Lowell, and Higginson—were light, or, if the topic became serious, he adopted a humorous tone or slipped the serious topic in under another less serious one. For example, while expounding on insanity, the autocrat slips in the topic of religion. The autocrat defines insanity as the "logic of an accurate mind overtasked." Good mental machinery, he argues, breaks if anything is thrust among its wheels and levers that stops them or reverses their motion. A weak mind, on the other hand, "does not accumulate force enough to hurt itself; stupidity often saves a man from going mad." Then the autocrat goes on to argue implicitly and humorously that orthodox religion will drive a strong mind insane: "Anything that is brutal, cruel, heathenish, that makes life hopeless for the most of mankind and perhaps for entire races,—anything that assumes the necessity of the extermination of instincts which were given to be regulated,—no matter by what name you call it . . . ought to produce insanity in every well-regulated mind" (42).

Just as William Ellery Channing's Unitarianism was only a step beyond Hutcheson's moral sense philosophy, so Holmes's rationalism, his faith in the human intellect to reject orthodox religion as outdated, represents the next logical stage of Unitarianism. Individual reason and knowledge, Holmes believed, were the grounds of social progress, whereas orthodox religion, particularly Calvinism with its original sin and predestination, stopped the wheels of progress. For Holmes, as for Channing, reason assumes morality, and men who are educated properly are naturally more moral than those who are uneducated.

Men who are educated properly go beyond mere facts or book knowledge. As the autocrat says, "Absolute, peremptory facts are bullies, and those who keep company with them are apt to get a bullying habit of mind; not of manners, perhaps; they may be soft and smooth, but the smile they carry has a quiet assertion in it, such as the Champion of the Heavy Weights . . . wears upon what he very inelegantly calls his 'mug.'" Scientific certainty "breeds a despotic way of thinking." It has "no spring in it, no courtesy, no possibility of yielding" (55).

Here Holmes equates facts with bullies, and people who dwell in facts with weightlifters. In this way, he cleverly interjects comments on social class, one of his favorite topics. Bullies are lower class as are weightlifters, as illustrated by the "inelegance" of calling one's face a "mug." The inference to be drawn is that facts are of a lower order of intelligence and those who use facts are lower in status than those who can interpret facts. In Holmes's hierarchy, facts, like books, should be used as stepping stones to higher thought.

About books the autocrat says, "I like books,—I was born and bred among them, and have the easy feeling, when I get into their presence, that a stable-boy has among horses. I don't think I undervalue them either as companions or instructors. But I can't help remembering that the world's great men have not commonly been great scholars, nor its great scholars great men. . . . [T]here are times in which every active mind feels itself above any and all human books" (131–32).

Too much book-learning and too many facts make people tedious. Those people who know how to use facts and books make the best company. And Holmes believed strongly, as he indicated in his discussion of Societies of Mutual Admiration, that men of intellect should come together to discuss books and ideas. As the autocrat says, "Society is a strong solution of books. It draws the virtue out of what is best worth reading, as hot water draws the strength of tea-leaves" (62). Steeping the leaves of books would both distill them and diffuse them, move them from the library into society where they could be used in conversation.

Conversation to Holmes is more than mere dialogue. It is a work of art like good music: "Talking is like playing on the harp; there is as much in laying the hand on the strings to stop their vibrations as in twanging them to bring out their music" (11). Later, Holmes has the autocrat say, "Some persons seem to think that absolute truth, in the form of rigidly stated propositions, is all that conversation admits. This is precisely as if a musician should insist on having nothing but perfect chords and simple melodies,—no diminished fifths, no flat sevenths, no flourishes, on any account . . . conversation must have its partial truths, its embellished truths, its exaggerated truths. It is in its higher forms an artistic product, and admits the ideal element as much as pictures or statues. One man who is a little too literal can spoil the talk of a whole tableful of men of *esprit*" (51–52). Emerson's "select society" and Holmes's Society of Mutual Admiration comprising "men of *esprit*" provided the antidote to fact-bullies and literal thinkers.

HIGGINSON'S LEGIBLE AUTHORITY

Of the four writers, Thomas Wentworth Higginson, a nineteenth-century social activist, clearly was the most radical. Too radical even for the liberal Christians at the First Religious Society of Newburyport, Higginson was forced to resign in 1848. The congregation claimed he preached only about slavery and politics. "My position as an Abolitionist," he wrote his mother, "they could not bear" (qtd. in Tuttleton 30). But abolition was not Higginson's only cause; he also advocated the rights of women, universal suffrage, temperance, and a ten-hour work day. Higginson did more than merely preach about these issues from the pulpit— he attended the State Temperance Convention in 1847, he petitioned for a national conference on women's rights, and, to the dismay of his Whig parishioners, he ran for Congress in 1848 as a Free Soiler. In addition, he was active in the Newburyport Lyceum, arranging lectures and entertaining speakers such as Emerson and Holmes. From 1852 to 1858, he served as pastor of the Free Church at Worcester, which he described as having no church membership or communion service, nor even calling themselves Christian, but instead resembling an ethical society (Tuttleton 33).

When the Fugitive Slave Law passed in 1850, Higginson, like Thoreau, advocated civil disobedience, but he was more active than Thoreau. He joined the Boston Vigilance Committee whose purpose was to protect fugitive slaves from pursuit and recapture. Attempting to free a captured runaway in 1851, Higginson lead an assault on the Boston Court House with axes, stones, and a battering ram. Later, he traveled to Kansas, met John Brown, and supported the futile raid on the arsenal at Harper's Ferry. While other Brown supporters—who, along with Higginson, were called the "Secret Six"—fled to Canada or elsewhere, Higginson stood firm and fully expected to be arrested. Yet even though his involvement was common knowledge, he was never arrested nor even called to Washington to testify in the investigation following the incident.

After the firing on Fort Sumter in 1861, the event that signaled the beginning of the Civil War, Higginson raised a group of volunteers from Worcester and was appointed captain of the Fifty-first Massachusetts Regiment, a commission he relinquished to become colonel of the First South Carolina Volunteers, the first regiment of ex-slaves in the Union army. Higginson held this command from November 1862 until May 1864. After leaving the army, though he continued to work for the causes in which he believed, Higginson concentrated on establishing himself as a writer, writing primarily history, biography, and literary and social criticism.

Where Emerson had his lecturing, Lowell his teaching, editorship, and diplomatic posts, and Holmes his teaching and medical practice, Higginson's only livelihood after the war was writing, and fortunately he became "one of the favorites" of James T. Fields, who took over the editorship of the *Atlantic* in 1859. According to Higginson, Fields offered him the "whole critical department" of the magazine, and though Higginson declined, he "wrote more largely for the first twenty volumes of the magazine than any other contributor except Lowell and Holmes" (*Cheerful Yesterdays* 186).

In early 1862, while Higginson was recruiting and drilling his regiment of volunteers, the *Atlantic* published his "A Letter to a Young Contributor," an article of advice to young writers who wanted their works published. After reading the article in Amherst, Emily Dickinson wrote to Higginson asking, "Mr. Higginson, Are you too deeply occupied to say if my verse is alive?" (qtd. in Tuttleton 143). Though Higginson advised Dickinson to delay publication until she had mastered conventional poetic form, he encouraged her writing through a correspondence that lasted until her death in 1886. At that time he and Mabel Loomis Todd coedited Dickinson's poems for publication, affixing titles, rearranging stanzas, and correcting grammar and usage.

Higginson's advice to Dickinson and his treatment of her poems can be illuminated by looking closely at his essays on writing and criticism. "A Letter to a Young Contributor" became what he calls a "little manual of literary composition," which he claims was urged into print several times by teachers, finally as a small book entitled *Hints on Writing and Speech-Making* (5). In the essay, though Higginson's voice is sometimes friendly, it is always authoritative as he discusses manuscript preparation and the role of the editor. For the greater part of the essay Higginson presents fairly typical advice about writing:

> Make sure the manuscript is neat and legible.
> Rewrite as often as necessary so that it needs no revision.
> Use a correct style but one that is not bland.
> Be neither too precise nor too lax.
> Write nobly, using no commonplaces.
> Don't use terms from other languages often.
> Study other languages, certainly, but "spare the raw material."
>
> (*Hints* 15–37)

This advice may not have been of much use to the novice writer, but it is written with such an authoritative voice, who could doubt its truth? Embedded in the tradition of Scottish and Unitarian rhetoric, Higginson's persuasive power relies on an ethos which assigns absolute authority to the father figure, who remains detached and "disinterested." The mythical father historically embodied in the priest, the preacher, and the professor, becomes in Higginson's essays the literary man and the editor. As the literary man—and Harvard graduate, minister, lecturer, and writer—Higginson assumes possession of knowledge that he is willing to impart only partially. The didacticism of voice and the incompleteness of information create a paternalistic authority that, to use Richard Sennett's term, can be described as "egoistic benevolence" (71). Readers who try to take Higginson's advice are confronted with questions to which he provides no answers: How often is it necessary for one to rewrite? What exactly is the distinction between an agreeable and an amusing tone or between correctness and blandness?

In the publication industry, the editor assumes the role of authoritative and disinterested father. But while he can "father" writers, he must also serve the interests of the publishers/owners and the readers/subscribers. As editor, Lowell tried to juggle these interests but was not always successful. For example, he once struck what he considered to be an offensive sentence in an article Thoreau wrote for the *Atlantic*. Thoreau, refusing to accept the editor's authority, accused Lowell of being a coward, afraid of "the utterance of a sincere thought" (Duberman 170). In this case, Thoreau resisted the "egoistic benevolence" of the editor and thus refused to legitimize his authority. Higginson, however, accepted without question the editor's authority.

He explains that editors face the difficult task of distinguishing between good writing and bad, of "drawing the line," and thus of setting the standard. Once that standard is fixed, Higginson writes, it must "be enforced without flinching" (*Hints* 11). Given his interest in antislavery causes, it is surprising that Higginson missed that to "enforce without flinching" sounds more like a task performed by an overseer with a whip than an editor with a pencil. To "enforce without flinching" Higginson believes is difficult but necessary in order to uphold standards. "Standards" thus becomes substituted for what in fact is expediency in the service of market capitalism. The term "standards," when spoken in the voice of the benevolent and disinterested father, belongs to the vocabulary of genteel rhetoric.

Higginson writes that the editor has "educated his eye till it has become microscopic, like a naturalist's, and can classify nine out of ten specimens by one glance at a scale or a feather" (*Hints* 14). The editor's "educated eye" resembles the penetrating imperial eye of Emerson's author/genius. The editor with his "educated eye" thus becomes mythicized as agent of authority and enforcer of standards that often remain illusory to ordinary writers. Nevertheless, Higginson argues, writers should not plead the merits of their own writing or point out the faults of other writing the editor has published, but instead should acquiesce to the editor's judgment and standards. Higginson's total submission to the authority of the editor may explain why he was so frequently published.

Despite Higginson's promotion and practice of genteel rhetoric, other rhetorics creep in. Blending genteel rhetoric with the rhetoric of market economy, he advises writers, "Be *noble* both in the *affluence* and the *economy* of your diction; spare no *wealth* that you can put in, and tolerate no superfluity that can be struck out" (italics mine, *Hints* 28). Later, he reminds them that "*cheap work* is usually *poor work*" (italics mine, *Hints* 45). Comparing the inventor of machines to the writer, Higginson asserts, "We unconsciously demand of our writers the same dash and the same accuracy that we demand in railroading or dry-goods jobbing" (*Hints* 33–34). Though Higginson ignores that the requirements of the writing marketplace often clashed with the standards of genteel paternalism, his rhetoric reveals the increasing tension between the two. While the Boston writers wanted to sell their ideas and their writing, they also wanted to create social and intellectual distance from the general reading public. Thus they wrote themselves as authorities of high culture and in the process institutionalized the sort of genteel rhetoric that Higginson practices.

Because writers are often more highly cultivated than their readers, Higginson perceives the writer's role to be cultivator and educator of public taste. Where Edward Channing had argued that writers should not "write down to [the public's] capacity and taste," Higginson argued that, to some extent, they must. He characterizes the reading public as "this vast, unimpassioned, unconscious tribunal, this average judgment of intelligent minds" that "criticizes" far beyond what it "can attain" (*Hints* 23). In order to sell writing, then, the writer must make his or her writing "attractive" and vital. The writing of William Ellery Channing, he argues, established the standard of the "pure and the colorless." This kind of writing simply will not sell in the modern magazine marketplace. Higginson encourages instead writing that is "saturated with warm life and delicious association [so] that every sentence shall palpitate, and thrill with the mere fascination of the syllables" (*Hints* 18).

One might think from reading these statements that Higginson, repudiating the rhetoric of William Ellery Channing, advocates a creative, flamboyant writing style. On the contrary, he admonishes writers to be more "modest" than individualist: "Have faith enough in your own individuality to keep it resolutely down for a year or two. . . . Premature individualism commonly ends either in a re-action against the original whims, or in a mannerism which perpetuates them" (*Hints* 29). Mannerism, he maintains, "imprisons us in novel fascination, yet we soon grow weary, and then hate our prison forever" (*Hints* 30).

Mannerism in writing meant to Higginson, as to Emerson, a lapse into superficiality, the writer as poseur. Where manners were signs of cultivation, mannerism represented its perversion. Higginson laments, "So few men in any age are born with a marked gift for literary expression, so few of this number have access to high culture, so few even of these have the personal nobleness to use their powers well, and this small band is finally so decimated by disease and manifold disaster, that it makes one shudder to observe how little of the embodied intellect of any age is left behind" (*Hints* 46–47). Higginson's rhetoric reveals a bias that presupposes that literary and critical production belong to the realm of the educated male elite, the benevolent fathers of American writing—an endangered group that embodied the intellect of the age. Emerson helped perpetuate that same notion.

In "Manners," Emerson envisions a "select society" composed of well-bred gentlemen who are good-natured and intelligent. The most important characteristic of "good breeding," according to Emerson, is "deference," which he explains thus: "Let us not be too much acquainted. . . . We should meet each morning, as from foreign countries, and spending the day together, should depart at night, as into foreign countries. In all things I would have the island of a man inviolate. Let us sit apart as the gods, talking from peak to peak all around Olympus" (*Essays* 292).

These writers' discussions about mannerism in writing reveal a desire for a writing identity that is stable and unchanging, controlled and in control. Such an identity assumes a hierarchical order, an understanding of one's place within that order, and a public reputation based on one's social standing. The distinction between manners and mannerism in writing is the distinction between authenticity—the stable self—and inauthenticity—the posing self. Manners manifested as modesty and deference serve as evidence of gentility, whereas "premature individualism" indicates impertinence, an unwillingness to observe prescribed forms, or, worse, an ignorance of the forms. More important, "premature individualism" figures as a refusal to legitimize the authority of gentility as embodied in the intellectual and benevolent father.

In Higginson's essay "The Cant of Cosmopolitanism," "mannerism" takes the form of cosmopolitanism, which, he argues, often is confused with good manners. Higginson perceives cosmopolitanism as ornament, something belonging to the "untravelled" or those who have traveled little (*Book and Heart* 110). Manners, Higginson asserts, are not a "matter of veneering, but ingrain" (*Book and Heart* 113). The basis of manners are self-respect and self-control. He admonishes writers to "get the real qualities . . . whether of social manners or of literary style, and all the rest shall be added unto you" (*Book and Heart* 115).

Higginson's mixing of manners and literature is intentional. Despite his democratic tendencies, Higginson had a real fear of leveling democracy. Though he was a radical reformer, as evidenced by his work in abolition and women's suffrage, he also was preoccupied with the idea of a genteel class expressing itself through literature. In "Literature as an Art," published in the *Atlantic,* he laments "Even in our largest cities, there are scarcely the rudiments of a literary class, apart from the newspapers"— but journalism is not real literature; rather an "outlet for the leisure time of a literary man." Words, Higginson argues, should be used for something other than practical knowledge or for the "transportation of intelligence," as a "wheelbarrow carries brick." Otherwise a book is simply a commodity, valuable to the consumer and profitable to the producer, but not within the domain of literature (746).

The problem with American writing, according to Higginson, is lack of cultivation. A cultivated person has neither "gingerbread-work" on his house nor ornamentation in his writing. "Good taste simplifies," Higginson declares. "Men whose early culture was deficient are far more apt to be permanently sophomoric than those who lived through the sophomore at the proper time and place. The reason is, that the habit of expression, in a cultivated person, matures as his life and thought mature; but when a man has had much life and very little expression, he is confused by his own thoughts, and does not know how much to attempt or how to discriminate." Higginson is particularly critical of the writing of Walt Whitman: "It is no discredit to Walt Whitman that he wrote 'Leaves of Grass,' only that he did not burn it afterwards" ("Literature" 756).

Literary art demands two kinds of structure: the first, which Higginson calls "philosophical," refers to logic, system, and completeness. The second, the "artistic," implies the "education of the taste." In literature, structure must be accompanied by "humility," "self-restraint," "moderation of tone," "habitual under-statement," and "patience," all elements of the "artistic." Higginson complains that American literature lacks "quiet power." The effects produced are usually "sensational." The problem is that American writers look for originality in the externals, when what is needed in order to produce literary art is "fresh inspiration combined with cultivated taste" ("Literature" 748–56). Thus while Higginson characterizes the writing of William Ellery Channing as pure and colorless, he nevertheless reproduces the genteel rhetoric of the Channing brothers.

Linking cultivated taste with morality, Higginson argues that the "invigorating air of great moral principles must breathe through all our literature." Though America still has not produced great literature, Higginson finds the promise of literary art in New England because of its Puritan heritage. While Puritanism was too stern and arduous, eliminating all frivolity, it nevertheless provided the "tradition of absolute righteousness, as the immutable foundation of all" ("Literature" 754).

In the period immediately preceding the Civil War, these four Boston writers turned their Harvard/Boston/New England habitus to cultural capital by becoming entrepreneurial gentleman-writers whose ideas had wide-ranging effects on American culture and letters. They used their genteel writing practices to achieve a hegemonic symbolic power, the power to construct a reality. This kind of symbolic power is not individual but rather communitarian and consensual, depending, as Bourdieu argues, on a "homogenous conception of time, space, number, and cause." Their genteel rhetorical practices—instruments of knowledge, communication, morality, aesthetics, authority—became powerful ideological systems structuring class, race, and gender domination (*Language and Symbolic Power* 166–67). And because the writers and their systems operate in the spirit of disinterested benevolence and manners, they succeed in repressing and coopting the dominated.

3

Elevation and Degradation

*It takes a long apprenticeship to train a whole people to
reading and writing.*
                                        —Oliver Wendell Holmes

When a nineteenth-century Boston writer has successfully created himself as author and created a market for his written ideas, how does he view the people around him? I have discussed to some extent these four writers' views of the world. To Emerson, the world, as "other me," is natural and therefore naturally appropriated. When people are present in Emerson's other me, they are either the "representative men" of history and literature or the omnipotent members of one of his "select societies." Though Emerson traveled and lectured, he remained, as much as possible, detached from the masses. "Detached" describes many aspects of Emerson. Living in Concord, he was detached from Boston. In speaking and writing, he was detached by "aloofness," the same aloofness he so admired in Everett. Similarly, though Lowell and Holmes were teachers and Higginson a minister, these men were in positions of prestige and power, positions that provided them a certain insulation from common people. When Lowell writes the descriptive phrase, the "rich mother-earth of common folk," he does more to erase common people than to venerate them. Rather, he de-composes common people as decaying organisms useful for fertilizer (*Biglow Papers* xi).

Holmes needed people as audience; however, that "every man [is] his own Boswell" indicates that a man could praise or flatter himself or join a Society of Mutual Admiration where other men were also their own Boswells. Instead of a practicing medical doctor, Holmes became a professor whose subjects were students and cadavers. Higginson's forays into common humanity I will discuss later in some detail, but as a literary and cultural writer, he needed "children" to father. After he first visited Emily Dickinson in 1870, he wrote his wife, "I never was with anyone who drained my nerve power so much. Without touching her, she drew from me. I am glad not to live near her" (qtd. in Edelstein 343–44). Higginson obviously found Dickinson unsatisfactory as child.

The genteel rhetoric of these writers, a rhetoric that successfully separated culture from people, was appropriate only for certain audiences and for certain topics. Its purpose, cultivating high culture, was to elevate humanity. But how much of humanity was capable of elevation? Were there those whose condition was so degraded that they could not elevate themselves nor be assisted in the effort? Were there those who degraded themselves by their rhetoric? The rhetoric of these writers drastically changed as they attempted to move out of their high-cultural domain and come to grips with the Other, in this case, immigrants, laborers, abolitionists, slaves.

After 1845, Boston's immigrant population began to grow rapidly. Though there were French, German, and Jewish immigrants, the largest new immigrant group was Irish (Solomon 5). This influx created a labor force for industry, particularly the growing textile industry, which with the invention of the sewing machine was becoming increasingly mechanized, requiring less skill from the workers. Martin Green notes that in 1849 textile industrialists ignored a tailors' strike and replaced the strikers with Irishmen who could run the machines. As Boston textile workers' output increased until it surpassed New York's, Boston wages nevertheless remained far below New York wages (Green 45). The rising immigrant population and low wages intensified urban problems such as crowded tenements, public drunkenness, prostitution, illness, and disease, problems the New England elite could scarcely ignore. The Irish were particularly troublesome as indicated by the following statement of Charles Francis Adams, Jr.: "Quick of impulse, sympathetic, ignorant and credulous, the Irish race have as few elements in common with the native New Englander as one race of men well can have with another" (qtd. in Solomon 29).

If immigration presented problems for the elite, slavery was even more pressing. Publishing the first number of the *Liberator* in 1831, William Lloyd Garrison shocked Bostonians by writing in a style that was immoderate and unrefined. "On the subject of slavery," he wrote, "I do not wish to think, or speak, or write, with moderation. No! no! Tell a man whose house is on fire to give a moderate alarm; tell him to moderately rescue his wife from the hands of the ravisher; tell the mother to gradually extricate her babe from the fire into which it has fallen,—but urge me not to use moderation in a cause like the present. I am in earnest—I will not equivocate—I will not excuse—I will not retreat a single inch—*and I will be heard*" (qtd. in M. Howe 252). Garrison's ungenteel rhetoric was, as he promised, "harsh" and "uncompromising." It stood in direct opposition to the rhetorical style taught at Harvard and traditionally practiced by the male New England elite.

Though Garrison shocked and dismayed Bostonians, he and other abolitionists forced them to confront the issue of slavery, though they confronted it reluctantly and abstractly. Slavery, after all, was fundamentally bound to the economic interests of Boston textile manufacturers, who sought business arrangements with Southern slaveholders and bought Southern cotton. These same manufacturers supported the arts, literary magazines, libraries, lecture series, and Harvard College. If Emerson, Holmes, Lowell, and Higginson intended to make their living lecturing and writing, they needed to maintain amiable ties with the monied manufacturers. Furthermore, these writers considered "manners" in speaking and writing very important. They were not Garrison, could not be Garrison. The self they cultivated and produced in their speaking and writing embodied the characteristics Edward T. Channing had taught them—disinterestedness and moderation—characteristics that stood in opposition to Garrison's unmannered rhetoric.

Though refusing to discuss the topic for several years, William Ellery Channing finally decided in 1836 that he should speak out about the institution of slavery. He obviously had Garrison in mind when he wrote that "to espouse a good cause is not enough. We must maintain it in a spirit answering to its dignity." Abolitionists must remember that "sympathy with the injured and oppressed may do harm, by being partial, exclusive and bitterly indignant" (*Slavery* 4). Channing believed that while slavery should be discussed and written about, it should be done in such a way so as "not to put in jeopardy the peace of the Slave-holding States." We "may not, must not, by rashness and passion increase the peril. To instigate the slave to insurrection is a crime for which no rebuke and no punishment can be too severe." Channing calls this kind of instigation "unholy interference" (*Slavery* 5).

Forbidding slaves to "lift an arm in [their] own defense" means that "our moral power" must be exerted on their behalf (*Slavery* 6). Nevertheless, we should not judge slaveholders too harshly. Channing carefully notes that he does not "intend to pass sentence on the character of the slave-holder." He argues that "Men are not always to be interpreted by their acts or institutions." What he intends to do instead of condemning slaveholders is "settle great principles" regarding slavery (*Slavery* 12). The principle argument against holding a man as property is that "he is a Rational, Moral, Immortal Being" created in God's image, whose purpose is "to unfold godlike faculties, and to govern himself by a Divine Law written on his heart" (*Slavery* 25).

It is the "fundamental law of our nature, that all our powers are to improve by free exertion. Action is the indispensable condition of progress to the intellect, conscience, and heart." If a human being is owned by another, then the proprietor has "the right to repress the powers of his slaves, to withhold from them the means of development, to keep them within the limits which are necessary to contentment in chains" (*Slavery* 28). Thus slavery strips a man of his fundamental right to "inquire into, consult, and seek his own happiness. His powers belong to another, and for another they must be used. He must form no plans, engage in no enterprises, for bettering his condition" (*Slavery* 51). The crux of Channing's argument is that the slave is denied the right of "developing his best faculties" (*Slavery* 52).

The capacity to develop faculties and improve, Channing believed, "allies him to the more instructed of his race, and places within his reach the knowledge and happiness of higher worlds. Every human being has in him the germ of the greatest idea in the universe, the idea of God; and to unfold this is the end of his existence" (*Slavery* 25–26). Since powers can be improved only by "free exertion," then the human being who is owned by another is denied the means to cultivate his faculties, the necessary condition of humanity (*Slavery* 28). Channing argues that

> Reason is God's image in man, and the capacity of acquiring truth is among his best inspirations. To call forth the intellect is a principal purpose of the circumstances in which we are placed, of the child's connection with the parent, and of the necessity laid on him in maturer life to provide for himself and others. . . . Now the whole lot of the slave is fitted to keep his mind in childhood and bondage. . . . Fed and clothed by others like a child, directed in every step, doomed for life to a monotonous round of labor, he lives and dies without a spring to his powers, often brutally unconscious of his spiritual nature. . . . His immortal spirit is systematically crushed.
>
> (*Slavery* 76–77)

In New England, Channing argues, people recognize their duty to instruct and elevate "their less favored brethren" through practicing benevolence. Here benevolence is "making perpetual encroachments on the domain of ignorance and crime. In communities, on the other hand, cursed with slavery, half the population, sometimes more, are given up, intentionally and systematically, to hopeless ignorance" (*Slavery* 79). Because the slaveowner has acquired a "lofty bearing from the habit of command over wronged and depressed fellow-creatures," he has cast away "true honor" (*Slavery* 93). In other words, slavery degrades both the slave and the slaveowner, or, in Channing's words, it passes the "sentence of perpetual degradation" (*Slavery* 79).

In 1854, Emerson also emphasizes the point that slavery degrades the slaveholder: "A man who steals another man's labor . . . steals away his own faculties; his integrity, his humanity is flowing away from him. The habit of oppression cuts out the moral eyes, and though the intellect goes on simulating the moral as before, its sanity is invaded, and gradually destroyed" (*Anti-Slavery Writings* 82–83). Argued in this way, slavery not only means degradation to the slaves, but also to all those who are implicated. Hutcheson and Reid had argued a century earlier that uncultivated faculties wither away. Channing and Emerson now argue that degradation of faculties occurs either by the inability to develop them (in the case of the slave), or by imposing one's will on another so that the other cannot develop (in the case of the slaveowner).

According to Channing, though slavery is an ugly institution, it can be eradicated without resorting to ugliness—without "unholy interference." Peace should not be disturbed. While slaveowning should be condemned, slaveowners should not be. The slave should not rise against the master. Exactly how slaves were going to be liberated is not clear since for Channing the problem could be settled by moral principle. The core of Channing's moral argument is degradation—the inability of the slave to cultivate the moral and intellectual faculties. In his sermon "The Moral Argument Against Calvinism," Channing had argued that Calvinism was wrong because it denied human reason. Now, as he speaks out against the degradation of slavery, he expands that argument. Similarly, Emerson argues, "We are in this world for nothing else than Culture: to be instructed . . . in the laws of moral and intelligent nature" (*Anti-Slavery Writings* 84–85). The degraded condition of the slave prohibits culture. To Channing and to Emerson, much of what comprised culture was self-culture—learning about one's own nature and then trusting one's own reasoning capacity.

While Channing could argue against slavery from a comfortable distance and stand on abstract moral principles, he chose in 1838 and 1840 to speak to working-class white men on the topics of "Self-Culture" and "On the Elevation of the Laboring Classes." In these lectures William Ellery Channing uses rhetoric similar to that of his brother Edward T. Channing when Edward described the "modern orator" as "one of the multitude, deliberating with them upon common interests, which are well understood and valued by all" (*Lectures* 17). William Channing begins his address by asserting his alignment with the working class: "I attach myself to the multitude, not because they are voters and have political power, but because they are men (*Self-Culture* 20). He argues that work binds together all men in the community; since in Boston "we are all bred and born to work," he rightfully belongs to the "great fraternity of working men" (*Self-Culture* 12).

The formation of character, Channing tells his audience, requires that one experience "difficulties." Therefore, men should perceive "manual labor" as a "school in which men are placed to get energy of purpose and character." Channing disapproves of the general disposition of men to shun physical labor or to seek jobs that do not require hard work. This disposition will lead eventually to a "demoralization of the community," to "excessive competition," and to a "disastrous instability." Channing assures his audience that labor possesses "great dignity," providing "force to the will, efficiency, courage, the capacity of endurance, and of persevering devotion to far-reaching plans." Labor is a better condition for the reception of divine ideas than a "luxurious or fashionable life. It is even better than a studious life, when this fosters vanity, pride, and the spirit of jealous competition" ("Elevation" 324–27, 346).

The second reason that Channing is united with working men is that they share a common nature—they possess the "divine powers of the soul" (*Self-Culture* 14). Real greatness, he argues, has nothing to do with one's place in society, but rather with "force of soul." Force of soul comprises "force of thought"—the intellectual—and "force of principle"—the moral (*Self-Culture* 17). Since these human qualities are manifestations of the divine, men therefore possess "means of improvement, of self-culture," which Channing defines as "the care which every man owes to himself, to the unfolding and perfecting of his nature" (*Self-Culture* 20–21). Self-culture begins with "moral discipline," the seeking of truth in a disinterested fashion. When the pressure of selfishness is removed, Channing argues, "thought expands as by a natural elasticity" (*Self-Culture* 33). One important means of self-culture is the "control of the animal appetites. To raise the moral and intellectual nature, we must put down the animal" (*Self-Culture* 56).

He advises the working men that they should not seek public office nor try to unite their votes in order to "triumph over the more prosperous." He argues, "An individual is not elevated by figuring in public affairs, or even by getting into office. He needs previous elevation to save him from disgrace in his public relations. To govern one's self, not others, is true glory" ("Elevation" 329). Channing hopes that "these lectures, and other sources of intellectual enjoyment now opening to the public, will abate the fever of political excitement, by giving better occupation to the mind" ("Elevation" 330).

Channing acknowledges that "some men are more gifted than others, and are marked out for more studious lives." However, "the work of such men is not to do others' thinking for them, but to help them to think more vigorously and effectually. Great minds are to make others great. Their superiority is to be used, not to break the multitude to intellectual vassalage, not to establish over them a spiritual tyranny, but to rouse them from lethargy, and to aid them to judge for themselves" ("Elevation" 352).

Throughout his lectures to the working men, Channing uses the third person pronoun to refer to the men to whom he is talking. This use of the third person, a distancing strategy, implies that Channing is talking about somebody else, someone not in the audience. I wonder whether those men thought as they listened to Channing that he really might be discussing another group.

Despite his "analysis" of the "laboring classes," the genteel rhetoric of Channing's speeches to the working men unselfconsciously exemplifies the ethos of the New England intelligentsia, an ethos that is at once liberal and patriarchal. Channing asserts that all men (though not women) have access to divinity through reason and moral sentiment. In short, "all men are created equal." The key word, however, is "created," since if inborn faculties are not developed, they wither and become useless, or they become "corrupted" or "degraded." Degradation includes being controlled by passion or not putting "down the animal." If one becomes elevated by cultivating his faculties, then reason overpowers passion. Those men who have established self-discipline and self-control are further enabled to cultivate their intellectual and moral faculties. They are the men who, in Channing's terms, are "marked out for more studious lives" and who should guide and direct the less "studious."

In his lectures to the white working men, Channing's arguments are clear: that working-class men need highly cultivated men to direct them, that working-class men must work to control their animal appetites, that they must not rush their development, that they must overcome "difficulties" before becoming gentlemen, that they should not become public figures until they have become gentlemen, and that they must learn proper use of language before they can become gentlemen. Most important, Channing emphasizes that only certain men are capable of full cultivation.

Channing's blurring of distinctions among kinds of work enables him to disengage himself from conditions of power. He reasons that since intellectual labor is the same as manual labor, then all men who work are brothers. This logic reflects a benevolent and liberal appropriation that enables the appropriator to represent all workers, all classes of people. In a similar vein several years later, Thomas Wentworth Higginson attempts to represent America's classes by arguing the following: "A nation is tested not by watching the class which looks down, but by the class which looks up. In England the upper classes naturally and innocently look down, and the middle and lower classes look up. In the United States, the so-called upper class may or may not look down, but the rest do not look up, and this makes an ineradicable difference. The less favored may point with pride or gaze with curiosity, but they certainly do not manifest reverence for the mere social position" (*Book and Heart* 128).

In this passage Higginson implies either that lower classes in the United States are satisfied with their position in society because they do not "look up," or (note his use of "the so-called" upper class) that in the United States society is less class-based than in England. Yet by using the metaphors of looking up/looking down, Higginson reifies categories of class as well as asserts his own position as detached observer. If the reader knows that Higginson is himself a member of the "so-called upper class," then his position is called into question. One way of "looking down" is to represent the Other, to tell their story, to block their "narratives from forming and emerging," as Edward Said argues in *Culture and Imperialism* (xiii). Higginson represents the "less favored" in ways that serve his own interests and elevate his already privileged status.

Representing the Other with confidence, the four New England male writers that I discuss in this book, with the qualified exception of Emerson, failed to see that nineteenth-century entrepreneurial capitalism required unmitigated exploitation of workers whether they were free or slave. While under slavery the master had absolute control over the slave's body, industrial capitalism with its systems of coercion encouraged workers to become willing accomplices in their own exploitation. These systems of coercion included discipline, supervision, and habituation (Braverman 62–63). Channing's addresses to working-class men that encouraged self-discipline, self-control, and acknowledgment of needing better or more cultivated men as guides and teachers, served the interests of industrial capitalism. Channing's rhetoric thus helped maintain the already-established divisions between mind work/body work and managers/managed. Furthermore, the notion of elevating the laboring classes assumes that they are malleable, but, even worse, as Ronald Takaki points out, it assumes the characterization of the group as "child/savage," a typical characterization of both black and urban white, particularly Irish, workers (Takaki 115).

From Channing's "Self-Culture" to Emerson's "Self-Reliance" is no great leap. In "Self-Reliance" Emerson argues, "Nothing is at last sacred but the integrity of your own mind" (*Selected Prose* 75). Once you become self-cultured—know your own mind—then you learn to trust yourself. Once you trust yourself, you can sever your ties to society. To know is to be and to be is to be free. However, because people should be self-reliant, Emerson sneers at "this bountiful cause of Abolition" and at the "obligation to put all poor men in good situations" (*Selected Prose* 75). The Emerson of "Self-Reliance" would thus say to the worker and the slave, "You are your own responsibility. Elevate yourself. Free yourself."

Emerson wrote "Self-Reliance" in 1841. Between 1841 and 1850, several major events occurred that forced Emerson to rethink the issue of slavery. Admitting Texas to the Union in 1845 brought about war with Mexico, lasting from 1846 to 1848. Abolitionists contended that statehood for Texas and the war were part of the Slave Power's great conspiracy to extend slavery. The defeat of Mexico in 1848 set into motion intense debate over whether slavery should be allowed in the territories taken from Mexico, territories that included much of what is now called the Southwest. Henry Clay's Compromise of 1850 attempted to resolve the dispute over slavery. Supported by Massachusetts senator Daniel Webster, the Compromise admitted California as a free state, created the territories of Utah and New Mexico with the question of slavery to be decided by popular sovereignty, settled the boundary dispute between Texas and Mexico, and ended the slave trade in Washington, D.C. It also put into place a new Fugitive Slave Law.

The Fugitive Slave Law of 1850 called for the appointment of federal commissioners who would issue warrants to those suspected of being runaway slaves. Commissioners were to be paid ten dollars per case if the runaway was returned, five dollars if the runaway was freed. Citizens were instructed, under penalty of fine or imprisonment, to turn in suspected runaways. Runaways were denied a jury trial as well as the right to testify in their own behalf (see Foner and Garraty 209–10, 432–33).

The Fugitive Slave Law set off an uproar in Massachusetts. Writing in the Newburyport *Union* newspaper, Thomas Wentworth Higginson's dictum was simple: "DISOBEY IT!" (Edelstein 105). Emerson wrote in his journal," I will not obey it, by God" (qtd. in *Anti-Slavery Writings* xxxix). In April 1851 when thirty-five citizens of Concord asked Emerson to speak publicly on the topic, he accepted, and in May he delivered his first address on the Fugitive Slave Law.

Emerson was particularly appalled that citizens of Massachusetts were required by law to participate in the capture of runaway slaves: "[T]he whole wealth and power of Boston,—200,000 souls, and 180 millions of money,—are thrown into the scale of crime; and the poor black boy, whom the fame of Boston had reached in the recesses of a rice-swamp, or in the alleys of Savannah, on arriving here, finds all this force employed to catch him. The famous town of Boston is his master's hound. The learning of the Universities, the culture of elegant society, the acumen of lawyers, the majesty of the Bench, the eloquence of the Christian pulpit, the stoutness of Democracy, the respectability of the Whig party, are all combined to kidnap him" (*Anti-Slavery Writings* 56).

For Emerson, all people in Massachusetts had been degraded by this law:

> When I look down the columns at the title of paragraphs, "Education in Massachusetts," "Board of Trade," "Art Union," "Revival of Religion," what bitter mockeries! The very convenience of property, the house and land we occupy, have lost their best value, and a man looks gloomily on his children, and thinks "What have I done, that you should begin life in dishonor?" Every liberal study is discredited: Literature, and science appear effeminate and the hiding of the head. The college, the churches, the schools, the very shops and factories are discredited; real estate, every kind of wealth, every branch of industry, every avenue to power, suffers injury, and the value of life is reduced.
>
> (*Anti-Slavery Writings* 54–55)

Emerson argues that because the law "enacts the crime of kidnapping," it is immoral and "contrary to the primal sentiment of duty" that all men are born with (*Anti-Slavery Writings* 57–58). Emerson is clear about what individuals should do: "This law must be made inoperative. It must be abrogated and wiped out of the statute book; but, whilst it stands there, it must be disobeyed" (*Anti-Slavery Writings* 71).

Emerson had to speak against the Fugitive Slave Law because it was directed to New Englanders and to him. As long as the slavery problem remained in the South and far away from New England, Emerson and others could either ignore it or speak against it by resorting to abstract principles. But the Fugitive Slave Law brought the problem to Emerson's doorstep by insisting that New England citizens return runaway slaves, thus making all New Englanders accomplices to slaveholders. This turn of events Emerson could not abide. The law degraded *him*.

Yet despite the vehemence with which he spoke against the Fugitive Slave Law, Emerson was still reluctant to work for abolition. In a speech in New York in 1854, he provides an explanation. In this passage Emerson presents several reasons for being a reluctant speaker against slavery:

1. Public issues are "odious and hurtful."
2. The speaker for a cause meddles.
3. He leaves his own work.
4. The intellectual should engage with only his natural audience—students or scholars.

What does Emerson mean when he says that public issues are "odious and hurtful"? He doesn't mean simply "controversial." Since the "Divinity School Address" Emerson himself had been the subject of controversy, a controversy he inspired with his doctrine of the divinity of the individual. In addition, he was a "meddler" in that he talked to people about how they should live their lives, and he had been a "meddler" in Concord in 1851 when he spoke against the Fugitive Slave Law. But perhaps it would have been more "odious and hurtful" to Emerson to remain silent.

The reason for Emerson's reluctance to become an abolitionist, I suspect, is that he would not be doing his "own work" and that the people who came to listen to abolition speeches would be those people to whom he was not "related." Slavery was not Emerson's issue, and the audience was not Emerson's audience. Furthermore, to speak against slavery and abolition meant taking a stand against New England's powerful elite. While Emerson had always spoken against conformity and for individualism, he had spoken abstractly and philosophically, never concretely and materially. To speak against slavery necessitated speaking about the materiality of slavery. Slaveholding was a capitalist enterprise that exploited people in the worst way possible—it held them captive and forced them to work for free. While New England's enterprising elite were not themselves slaveholders, they were deeply involved in the slaveholding system by trading with slaveholders. The men who built and ran mills such as those in Lowell had become wealthy on cotton and, by implication, on the backs of slaves. These are the public issues Emerson refused to address.

Though Emerson finally did speak out strongly against slavery, he wanted, like William Ellery Channing, to join the cause with a "spirit of dignity" rather than with an "overbearing and defying spirit." "Let us withhold every reproachful, and, if we can, every indignant remark," he says. "In this cause, we must renounce our temper, and the risings of pride" (*Anti-Slavery Writings* 8). The abolition cause, Emerson eventually decided, needs highly cultivated gentlemen: "The theory of personal liberty must always appeal to the most refined communities and to the men of the rarest perception and of delicate moral sense. . . . A barbarous tribe of good stock will by means of their best heads secure substantial liberty. But when there is any weakness in race, as is in the black race, and it becomes in any degree a matter of concession and protection from their stronger neighbors, the incompatibility and offensiveness of the wrong will, of course, be most evident to the most cultivated" (*Anti-Slavery Writings* 80).

Though the wrongs may have been evident to the cultivated, most of the cultivated, including Emerson, were late in joining the movement. There were, however, important exceptions. Wendell Phillips, for example, was another Harvard graduate and student of Edward T. Channing, and the cousin of Oliver Wendell Holmes. Phillips had been an early supporter of Garrison, had helped to bring Frederick Douglass into the movement, and had written a letter that served as an introduction to *The Narrative of the Life of Frederick Douglass,* Douglass's first autobiography, published in 1845. Thomas Wentworth Higginson had spoken against slavery even from the pulpit and had served as Phillips's bodyguard on several occasions, protecting him not only from "rowdies, Democrats, and Negrophobes," but also from "prominent Boston lawyers, merchants, and brokers" (Edelstein 241). Another early abolitionist was Edmund Quincy, son of Josiah Quincy, the mayor of Boston and president of Harvard. But these "cultivated" men were hardly typical abolitionists.

Emerson's major argument against slavery was similar to William Ellery Channing's: slavery degrades individuals and society: "Slavery is no scholar, no improver; it does not love the whistle of the railroad; it does not love the newspaper, the mailbag, a college, a book, or a preacher who has the absurd whim of saying what he thinks; it does not increase the white population; it does not improve the soil; everything goes to decay" (*Anti-Slavery Writings* 21).

But Emerson delved deeper than Channing into the conditions of power, both the power of the slaveholder and the power of the Northern manufacturer. Regarding the slaveholder, he said, "We sometimes say, the planter does not want slaves, he only wants the immunities and the luxuries which the slaves yield him; give him money, give him a machine that will yield him as much money as the slaves, and he will thankfully let them go. He has no love of slavery, he wants luxury, and he will pay even this price of crime and danger for it. But I think experience does not warrant this favorable distinction, but shows the existence, beside the covetousness, of a bitterer element, the love of power, the voluptuousness of holding a human being in his absolute control" (*Anti-Slavery Writings* 17). Emerson recognized that the slave was more than money to the slaveholder; the slave's body was the site of absolute control, the kind of authoritative relationship a slaveholder could not have with a machine.

Emerson brought to the abolition movement a philosophical understanding of power as well as an understanding of the complicity of all who enjoyed the benefits of slave labor. In speaking about the latter, he uses the pronoun "we," thus implicating himself as well as Northern capitalists:

[W]e are shopkeepers, and have acquired the vices and virtues that belong to trade. We peddle, we truck, we sail, we row, we ride in cars, we creep in teams, we go in canals—to market, and for the sale of goods. The national aim and employment streams into our ways of thinking, our laws, our habits, and our manners. The customer is the immediate jewel of our souls. Him we flatter, him we feast, compliment, vote for, and will not contradict. It was . . . the dictate of trade, to keep the negro down. We had found a race who were less warlike, and less energetic shopkeepers than we; who had very little skill in trade. We found it very convenient to keep them at work, since, by the aid of a little whipping, we could get their work for nothing but their board and the cost of whips.

(*Anti-Slavery Writings* 20)

Emerson then drops the "we" and returns to the easier subject of the slaveholders: "One must look to the planters of the South with the same feelings that he would regard the spider and the fly, the tiger and the deer. It is a barbarism. The people are barbarous. They are still in the animal state. They are not accountable like those whose eyes have once been opened to a Christianity that makes a return to evil impossible. Revolutions, as we say, never move backward" (*Anti-Slavery Writings* 48). The fate of slaves, he argues, depends on the "raising of their masters." "Elevate, enlighten, civilize the semi-barbarous nations of South Carolina, Georgia, Alabama—take away from their debauched society the Bowieknife, the rum-bowl, the dice-box, and the stews—take out the brute, and infuse a drop of civility and generosity, and you touch those selfish lords with thought and gentleness. Instead of racers, jockies, duelists and peacocks, you shall have a race of decent and lawful men, incapacitated to hold slaves, and eager to give them liberty" (*Anti-Slavery Writings* 38). In this passage Emerson depicts Southerners as brutish, controlled by passion, and less than human.

Though Emerson had been doubtful of the capacity of slaves to improve or elevate themselves, he used the accomplishments of emancipated slaves in the British West Indies as evidence that the "negro race" was susceptible to "rapid civilization." Since the British had emancipated them in 1833, former slaves in the West Indies had made great strides: "If, before, he was taxed with such stupidity, or such defective vision, that he could not set a table square to the walls of an apartment, he is now the principal, if not the only mechanic . . . and is, besides, an architect, a physician, a lawyer, a magistrate, an editor, and a valued and increasing political power." Best of all, Emerson argued, "is the testimony to [former slaves'] moderation. They receive hints and advances from the whites. . . . They hold back, and say to each other, that social position is not to be gained by pushing" (*Anti-Slavery Writings* 30).

Here is another example of genteel rhetoric representing its rhetorical subjects as part of its desire to mold them. The "moderation" of West Indian ex-slaves assuages white fears about what might happen after emancipation in the United States. If the slaves of the West Indies can be taught to "receive hints and advances from the whites," then perhaps Southern slaves can also be taught to cultivate that trait.

Since the passage of the Fugitive Slave Law, the New England writers had been critical of Daniel Webster, considering him, after his capitulation to Clay's Compromise, a traitor to the Northern cause. But Emerson's criticism of Webster went deeper. He argued that Webster was particularly culpable because he was cultivated (though he was not from Harvard), and he had the power of language. Emerson characterizes him as the

> one eminent American of our time, whom we could produce as a finished work of nature. We delighted in his form and face, in his voice, in his eloquence, in his power of labor, in his concentration, in his large understanding. . . . He has been by his clear perception and statement in all these years, the best head in Congress, and the champion of the interests of the northern seaboard. . . . [Yet] on the 7th March 1850, in opposition to his education, association, and to all his own most explicit language for thirty years, he crossed the line, and became the head of the slavery party in this country. . . . He obeys his powerful animal nature. . . . He believes in so many words, that government exists for the protection of property. He looks at the Union as an estate, a large farm. . . . [H]e has no moral perception, no moral sentiment.
>
> (*Anti-Slavery Writings* 66–67)

Webster's action on the Fugitive Slave Bill was unforgivable not because of the mistake Webster had obviously made, but because of what he had symbolized to New Englanders. In Emerson's perception, he had thoroughly degraded himself.

James Russell Lowell had criticized Daniel Webster earlier, when Lowell had discovered that Webster's son was recruiting, with his father's approval, volunteers for the Mexican War. Calling Webster an "eagle turned buzzard," Lowell said that he could claim "only a bastard's inheritance in that sky where he should have soared supreme." His "great faculties" had been debased. Lowell's rhetoric, like Emerson's, is vitriolic because God had "bestowed upon this man that large utterance, that divine faculty of eloquent speech" (*Anti-Slavery Papers* 37). To these writers Webster was particularly culpable because he was so highly cultivated. By supporting the Mexican War and the Compromise of 1850, Webster had debased his faculties and his moral sentiment. That Webster had farther to fall than others made his fall even more absolute. To the New England intelligentsia, Webster's fall was so complete that they ceased describing politicians as having "power of character."

Though Emerson was fired into writing and speaking by the Fugitive Slave Law, Lowell became depressed and incapacitated by it. Since 1846 Lowell had been writing on slavery and abolition for the *National Anti-Slavery Standard,* the voice of the American Anti-Slavery Society. Like Emerson's wife Lidian, Lowell's wife Maria encouraged her husband's abolitionist writing. By 1850, however, Maria had borne four children in rapid succession, two of them having died within a year of their birth. Not surprisingly, Maria was in ill health, and James Russell, who was already depressed over the death of his children, was moved to despair over the Fugitive Slave Law. For these reasons, the family decided in 1851 to go to Europe to recuperate and escape the turmoil at home.

The European trip signaled a break in Lowell's abolition activities, and upon his return in late 1852, he wrote to Higginson that while he sympathized with any movement that aimed to "elevate man or woman socially or morally," he now believed that the "*How* must be left to the care of individual experience" (qtd. in Duberman 132). At that point, his enthusiasm for the cause of abolition having waned, Lowell wanted to devote his time to writing poetry and literature. His writings on abolition abruptly ceased.

But while he wrote, Lowell was an astute observer of the ironies of the movement. Since he was a student of words, his essays are often filled with word play. For example, in "A Word in Season," respectable conservatives become fanatics and reformers become true conservatives. "Evil, unaided by respectability," Lowell argues, "would shrink back to its original darkness before the first glance of the terrible eyes of the right. But the great inert mass of respectability lies all around it, like a rampart of insensate cotton bales, calling itself Conservatism" (*Anti-Slavery Papers* 4). Conservative respectability is also found in the abolition movement, as with the "poet who can round off a couplet," or the "editor who can give sound to the closing of a paragraph by some flourish about freedom and the destiny of America." But when abolition requires action rather than speculation, Lowell writes, "they repudiate immediately with indignation all sympathy with *fanaticism*, yet remain as good abolitionists as before" (*Anti-Slavery Papers* 5). Lowell implicitly argues that some abolitionist writers want merely to write for the cause, to advocate freedom as long as freedom remains an abstract principle. These abolitionists do not want to grapple with real problems or with real people.

In "The Prejudice of Color," Lowell calls color prejudice "chromatic *noblesse*" and derides those people who found notions of "nobility" on "no better distinction than an accidental difference in the secreting vessels of the skin." He also notes the irony of black men being "despised" though they have "endured unparalleled hardships and oppressions with resignation and patience," while "red men" are admired even though they have displayed "more hideous qualities than any other savages" (*Anti-Slavery Papers* 18). Lowell then launches into an argument about the superiority of the "African race": "We have never had any doubt that the African race was intended to introduce a new element of civilization, and that the Caucasian would be benefited greatly by an infusion of its gentler and less selfish qualities. The Caucasian mind, which seeks always to govern, at whatever cost, can never come to so beautiful or Christian a height of civilization, as with a mixture of those seemingly humble, but truly more noble, qualities which teach it to obey" (*Anti-Slavery Papers* 22).

In *The Black Image in the White Mind,* George Fredrickson uses this particular quotation from Lowell as an example of what he calls "romantic racialism"—the idea that the slave was naturally docile, gentle, kind, patient, and forgiving. The fictional version of the romanticized slave is Harriet Beecher Stowe's Uncle Tom. Fredrickson argues that because there had been no slave insurrections since the Nat Turner rebellion in 1831, abolitionists could romanticize the slave as naturally docile and thus combat the notion of the slave as "child" or "savage" (109). Nevertheless, in concluding the essay Lowell undercuts his arguments about the slave being more noble and more civilized than the Caucasian by writing, "Had we room we might easily prove by historical examples that no race has ever so rapidly improved by being brought into contact with a higher civilization (even under the most terrible disadvantages) as the one of which we have been speaking" (*Anti-Slavery Papers* 22). Lowell apparently was going to have it both ways: African slaves were superior to Caucasians (romanticization) and African slaves had been improved by contact with Caucasians (cultivation). Like the Scottish philosophers, Lowell mixed the ideal and the material.

The "African race" was the topic of much speculation. Were they as intelligent as whites? Were they naturally barbarous? Or were they, as Harriet Beecher Stowe depicted Uncle Tom, naturally docile? Did whites and blacks have the same origin? Many of the New England elite looked to the scientific theories of Louis Agassiz, the Swiss-born zoologist. After lecturing for the Lowell Institute in 1846, Agassiz had been appointed professor of natural history at Harvard in 1847, and he was also a member of the prestigious Saturday Club with Emerson, Lowell, and Holmes. In his theory of the origin of races, Agassiz, like Lowell, seemed to waffle. He argued that the different races were created in their present habitats. Though races did not have a common origin, race origin represented "a superior order, established from higher and considerate views, by an intelligent Creator" (qtd. in Stanton 106).

Agassiz wanted to make clear that his theory did not conflict with scripture. Genesis does not mention Indians, Mongolians, or Hottentots; therefore, "if we find that these peoples are not descended from Adam and Eve, we shall not have contradicted Genesis" (qtd. in Stanton 107). Agassiz, I suppose, assumed that Adam and Eve were Caucasian. Restating Agassiz's theory in 1860, another scientific writer explained that each race is "constituted to flourish best in a climate akin to its native one" (qtd. in Fredrickson, *Black Image* 137–38). Since the Caucasian originated in and thrived in temperate regions, and the African originated in and thrived in the tropics, this theory raised considerable doubt about the African's destiny in the United States, at least in the Northern states.

Oliver Wendell Holmes was the only one of the four writers who did not write about slavery or abolition. However, he has the autocrat comment offhandedly, "Now look at what is going on in India,—a white, superior 'Caucasian' race against a dark-skinned, inferior, but still 'Caucasian' race—and where are English and American sympathies? We can't stop to settle all the doubtful questions; all we know is, that the brute nature is sure to come out most strongly in the lower race, and it is the general law that the human side of humanity should treat the brutal side as it does the same nature in the inferior animals,—tame it or crush it" (*Autocrat* 66). In this passage, even wearing the mask of the autocrat, Holmes cannot deny his straightforward, hateful language. There is no "double consciousness" here; the writer is unconscious of the violent language that exposes the "brutal side" of his own nature.

In 1850, while Holmes was dean of Harvard Medical School, three young black men came to Holmes requesting admission. Two of the men were sponsored by the Massachusetts Colonization Society and planned to take their medical careers to Liberia. The third man was Martin Robinson Delaney from Pittsburgh, who, though he came with high recommendations, had been rejected by several medical schools because he was black. Holmes admitted all three men. When the black men attended class, the white students refused to talk with them or sit near them. Eventually the white students met and passed several resolutions, among them the following: "Resolved That we have no objection to the education and evaluation of blacks but do decidedly remonstrate against their presence in College with us" (qtd. in Hoyt 149).

After consulting with other faculty members, Holmes met with the black students and informed them that, having paid their fees, they could stay until the end of the semester but could not continue thereafter. Holmes was not about to endanger his own career to "elevate" black men. Perhaps he agreed with one of the white students who, in a letter to the Boston *Journal*, protested the admission of the blacks because of their "inferior mental ability" (qtd. in Hoyt 150). Martin Delaney never got his medical degree, but instead was active in the abolition movement and in the underground railroad, and was a writer (briefly) for Frederick Douglass's *North Star*, a recruiter for the Union in the Civil War, and eventually a major in the Union Army.

While Emerson was agonizing over the issues and Holmes and Lowell were building their writing and teaching careers, Higginson not only was writing about reform but also was practicing it. From 1850 to 1854, he ran unsuccessfully for Congress on the Free Soil ticket; he formed in Newburyport a free evening school for factory workers and directed the school's female department; he preached in Worcester as minister of the Free Church; he delivered speeches on temperance, women's rights, and abolition; and he became an active member of the Boston Vigilance Committee, a secret committee formed to help free those blacks taken into custody under the Fugitive Slave Law.

In 1854 when the fugitive Anthony Burns was seized and jailed at the Court House, Higginson led an attack on the Court House with a fourteen-foot battering ram and axes. During the fray, a guard was killed and Higginson's chin was slashed by a cutlass. Though the attack was unsuccessful and Burns was returned to the South, Higginson became a hero to the abolitionists who did not agree with the Garrisonian nonviolent approach to abolition.

After the Burns affair, Higginson began to imagine for himself a life as a militant but prestigious revolutionary. He writes in his journal, "The men now arrested are obscure men; *their* sufferings will be of comparatively little service; but I have a name, a profession, & the personal position which make my bonds a lesson & a stimulus to the whole country. What better things could I do for liberty? What so good?" (qtd. in Edelstein 160). In a sermon Higginson told his parishioners at the Free Church that "calm irresistible force, in a good cause, becomes sublime. . . . I can only make life worth living for, by becoming a revolutionist" (qtd. in Edelstein 162).

Higginson's desire to become a "revolutionist" spills over into his writing. In June and August of 1861, respectively, the *Atlantic* published Higginson's essays "Denmark Vesey" and "Nat Turner's Insurrection." Instead of praising slaves' meekness, docility, and Christian forgiveness as Lowell and Stowe had done, Higginson praises their guile and their militancy. In "Denmark Vesey," he is impressed with the secrecy, the "thoroughness of organization," and the "boldness of conception" that led to the 1822 insurrection in Charleston, South Carolina. The leader, Denmark Vesey, was a free man, a former Haitian slave who had sailed the world with his master Captain Vesey, purchased his own freedom in 1800, and settled in Charleston where he worked as a carpenter and, according to his accusers, endeavored to "embitter the minds of the colored population against the white" (730). Believing that slavery was "contrary to the laws of God," Vesey argued that "slaves were bound to attempt their emancipation, however shocking and bloody might be the consequences" (731).

Vesey habitually rebuked men who were obsequious to whites. When they "answered, 'We are slaves,' he would sarcastically and indignantly reply, 'You deserve to remain slaves.'" When asked what they could do, Vesey tells the slaves to go get a "spelling-book" and read about Hercules (731). Higginson reports that "Vesey was known to be for a war of immediate and total extermination," and when some of his men protested that they should spare women and children, Vesey replied that "it was for their safety not to leave one white skin alive" (735).

The insurrection, Higginson points out, was conceived and organized "without the slightest cooperation from any white man" (737) and even after the leaders were caught, tried, and convicted, their "self-control . . . did not desert them." Vesey's lieutenant Peter Poyas, for example, reportedly told the convicted slaves, "Do not open your lips; die silent as you shall see me do" (740).

Where Higginson describes Denmark Vesey and Peter Poyas as brave and cunningly intelligent, in "Nat Turner's Insurrection," he portrays Turner as having strong "moral faculties." He "never had been known to swear an oath, to drink a drop of spirits or to commit a theft" (174). He knew "no book but his Bible, and that by heart" (185). Yet Turner led a band of slaves from house to house in Southampton County, Virginia, eventually killing about sixty white men, women, and children— "nothing that had a white skin was spared" (176). Higginson concludes the essay by recounting the reports of other insurrections that followed Turner's rebellion, the "terrors that came back from nine other Slave States as the echo of the voice of Nat Turner" (183). In this essay, Higginson caters to the fear of Southern whites that "a Nat Turner might be in every family" and that the "same bloody deed might be acted over at any time and in any place" (186).

The rhetoric Higginson uses to represent the black insurrectionists is not the rhetoric of degradation. In neither essay do blacks degrade themselves by reverting to a brute or savage state. But neither do the acts of violence they commit elevate them. Higginson's Vesey and Turner already have elevated themselves by becoming highly literate: Vesey is eloquent in his intelligent aphorisms, Turner in his heart-knowledge. In Higginson's inventions, violence legitimizes their manhood. It restores their manly dominance by rendering them forever masterless. Vesey and Turner become Higginson's fantasized black versions of Emersonian self-reliant men. But rather than freeing themselves through civilizing knowledge, they free themselves by inflicting violence upon "white skin."

Unlike Higginson, who wrote about people, Emerson always argued from definition and principle. In April of 1862, a year after Confederate troops fired on Fort Sumter and ignited the Civil War, Emerson's "American Civilization" was published in the *Atlantic*. Emerson begins by defining civilization as a "degree of progress" from rude states when people dwelled in caves or trees like apes or cannibals. Defining by negation, Emerson argues that a "nation that has no clothing, no alphabet, no iron, no marriage, no arts of peace, no abstract thought, we call barbarous." Conversely, civilization is a site where men are capable of reason and morality and therefore of high "organization," "supreme delicacy," "religion, liberty, sense of honor, and taste" (502). It is a place where the division of labor is practiced so that "each man" may "choose his work according to his faculty" and where the "diffusion of knowledge" takes place.

The "vital refinements," Emerson argues, are morality and intellect, and the test of civilization is whether a country produces a moral individual who through reason and industry forms societies of mutual interest such as kinship, trade, and "habitual hospitality" (506). Emerson uses the metaphor of a modern ship to underscore the complexity and rationalization of skill that he considers the underpinning of civilization. As the ship relies on "compass and chart," "lunar observation," and "chronometer," so the civilized nation relies on the "man who maintains himself," the "farm made to produce all that is consumed on it," and the "prison made into a reform school and a manufactory of honest men out of rogues" (503–4).

The highest proof of civilization is the government that operates to secure the "greatest good of the greatest number" and enables all "honest men" to "earn their bread by their industry." By "denying a man's right to his labor," the Southern states have "introduced confusion into the moral sentiments of their people." Because slaveholders are permitted to eat the "fruit of other men's labor," they have effectively "pronounced labor disgraceful." Thus the United States actually comprises two states of civilization: a "higher state where labor and the tenure of land and the right of suffrage are democratical, and a lower state in which the old military tenure of prisoners or slaves and of power and land in a few hands makes an oligarchy" (506–7). The existence of the nation is menaced by the South's disorder, which Emerson calls "Africanization." He predicts that the entire country will be "Africanized" if Southern disorder is not replaced by the Northern order of rationalized industry—the "best civilization" (506–7). Thus, for Emerson the project of emancipation becomes the larger project of extending New England civilization to the South.

Several years earlier when Lowell was still writing essays for the abolition movement, he wrote the following fable that uses Siamese Twins as metaphors for North and South:

Once upon a time Chang took to bad courses. He frequented bar-rooms and even more disreputable places, and at last became an inveterate sot. Now wherever Chang went, of course Eng was seen also, and his character began to suffer accordingly. Nor was this all. Whatever diseases Chang contracted, Eng suffered his share of, not to mention that, though a cold-water man himself, his liver was being burnt up by the brandy which ran down his brother's throat. Eng consulted his spiritual adviser, and wished him to reason with Chang and represent to him the wickedness of his conduct. "It would not do, my dear sir, it would not do at all. Mr. Chang is a member of my society and subscribes liberally for missions and other gospel purposes." Eng went to his lawyer. That gentleman merely laid his finger on the bond which held the two brothers together, and shook his head. In despair Eng sent for a surgeon. "I would not venture an operation, lest both parties bleed to death." One day Eng was sitting on the edge of the gutter into which his brother had tumbled, when a medical man, thought rather *ultra* by the faculty, came up. Eng looked at him despairingly. "Give him his choice, as soon as he is sober, to begin a reform tomorrow morning, or to submit to the knife at once. In a few months the operation will be necessary to save your life." (*Anti-Slavery Papers* 156–57)

In Lowell's fable, the Siamese twins figure as the problem of the Union. Should the twins remain together or should they separate even at the cost of both dying? The rhetorical strategy of using Siamese twins and giving them Asian names defamiliarizes the problem for readers and establishes the feasibility of solving the problem medically. In obvious reference to Holmes, as the "medical man," the surgeon decides that an operation will be necessary. In this way, the complexities of the problem become simplified as medical necessity. Disunion was necessary in order to protect New England from the degraded and "Africanized" South.

At the beginning of the Civil War, these four writers agreed on the superiority of their own cultivation and that of New Englanders in general. But their views diverged when they considered how best to civilize and elevate others. Holmes refused to make public pronouncements except through the autocrat or another persona. Lowell retreated into the respectability of Harvard professor who, despite his earlier fable that advocated "the knife," was no longer interested in revolution. Emerson perceived war as a first stage in the long process of civilizing both master and slave. Higginson, however, was already raising volunteers and drilling them in anticipation of violent, regenerative battle.

4

Rhetoric and War

One great principle, which we should lay down as immovably true, is that if a good work cannot be carried on by the calm, self-controlled, benevolent spirit of Christianity, then the time for doing it has not come.
—William Ellery Channing

We are afraid of our own principles as a raw recruit of his musket.
—James Russell Lowell

Rhetoric and war historically have been so completely interrelated that rhetorical terms are also terms of battle and conquest. Thus rhetoric is used to defend one's position and to conquer one's adversary or one's audience. Armed with words as weapons, speakers and writers attack their opponents by marshaling their arguments. The speaker or writer who states the strongest case wins and the opponent yields. In the *Rhetoric,* Aristotle writes that "it is absurd to hold that a man ought to be ashamed of being unable to defend himself with his limbs, but not of being unable to defend himself with speech and reason." He adds that the "use of rational speech is more distinctive of a human being than the use of his limbs" (1355b). In other words, Aristotle believed that conquest by words is a better way to win than by "limbs." To resort to the physical in order to conquer meant that rhetoric had broken down or had been exhausted. Using the Civil War as context, this chapter explores the connections between words and violence. When are words capable of postponing physical violence? When do words provoke violence? Might words in certain contexts be considered as having already committed violence? I ask these questions as I examine the words of Boston intellectuals who considered themselves as epitomizing high culture. I ask what happens to genteel rhetoric when it confronts the realities of brutalizing war.

Agreeing with Aristotle about the superiority of words as means of conquest, William Ellery Channing argued that while certain "energies of mind" were called forth by military action, military men could not be geniuses of the "highest order" (*Discourses* 154). Under the rule of the military, the human intellect, Channing believed, would lose its "thirst for progress" and would "fall back towards barbarism" (*Discourses* 164). True heroism, the "heroism of intellect and conscience," belongs to "virtuous, elevated minds, which shall consecrate themselves to the work of awakening in men a consciousness of the rights, powers, purposes, and greatness of human nature" (*Discourses* 170). War, the manifestation of small and evil minds, Channing believed, had been replaced by human improvement and the "just, impartial, disinterested principles of Christianity" (*Discourses* 79, 87, 93). True to his gospel of Christian progress, Channing argued simply that individual moral sense would indubitably eliminate violence and war, replacing them with universal benevolence.

The young lawyer Charles Sumner, who had studied rhetoric under Edward T. Channing at Harvard, fell under the influence of William Ellery Channing's notions of pacifism and social reform, though he seemed not to have understood the doctrine of Christian benevolence. In 1840 Sumner joined a discussion group that met weekly at Channing's house on Mount Vernon Street. After Channing's death in 1842, Sumner, determined to improve society, became active as a social reformer. Sumner perceived reform, however, not as concerned with individual human suffering but rather with "the good of the whole human family, its happiness, its development, its progress" (qtd. in Donald 105). In other words, like Channing he was certain that social reform should be founded upon abstract and universal principles. But Sumner lacked Channing's ethical appeal. He failed to realize that reformers speak to real people, and though they might argue from principle, they must pay close attention to the audience on whom they depend for adherence. The audience must accept the values embedded within the principles or at least be open to accepting those values.

In *The New Rhetoric*, Perelman and Olbrechts-Tyteca maintain "For argumentation to exist, an effective community of minds must be realized" (14). When William Ellery Channing spoke to the working-class men about elevation, he attempted to speak to them as one of them, to establish a "community of minds." The extent to which he succeeded is open to debate, but his discourse indicates that he understood that he must try. In contrast, Sumner proved to be notoriously insensitive to his audiences.

In 1845, he was invited to deliver Boston's Fourth of July Oration, an occasion for celebrating the Revolutionary War and its heroes. Ignoring the aim of the occasion as well as the number of men wearing military uniforms in his audience, Sumner announced his theme: "In our age there can be no peace that is not honorable. There can be no war that is not dishonorable" (Donald 109). Then for two hours Sumner voiced William Ellery Channing's pacifist views and concluded that the "grandeur of nations" lies not in warfare but in "moral elevation, enlightened and decorated by the intellect of man" (qtd. in Donald 110). The "community of minds" that listened to Sumner, however, did not share his views. Sumner had failed to consider the basic rhetorical principles of audience, occasion, and purpose. He failed to understand that rhetorical aims are achieved not only by erudition and logical argumentation but also by what his former teacher Edward T. Channing called the "power of character," or ethical appeal. The Fourth of July Oration was not the last instance where Sumner's rhetoric demonstrated not only gross insensitivity but also utter hostility toward his auditors.

At the formation of the Free Soil party in 1848, Sumner, after lengthy balloting, was elected in 1851 to the U.S. Senate, a post he held for the remainder of his life. In 1854, he helped reform the Republican party, a party that fused Free Soilers and antislavery Whigs. As senator, Sumner stood as an uncompromising opponent of slavery. Slavery became Sumner's cause and the Senate floor his platform for social reform. As senator, however, Sumner abandoned his pacifist stance as his rhetoric became increasingly militant.

In 1854, Illinois senator Stephen A. Douglas introduced and implemented the passage of the Kansas-Nebraska Act that repealed the 1820 Missouri Compromise prohibiting the spread of slavery to the northwestern territories. Conservative Northerners and supporters of Daniel Webster had believed the Compromise of 1850, which included the Fugitive Slave Act, was necessary in order to save the Union, but now under the Kansas-Nebraska Act they faced the possibility of new slave states in the West. The passage of the Kansas-Nebraska Act set off such an uproar in the North that Douglas, going home to Illinois by train, remarked that he could travel from Boston to Chicago by the light of his own effigy (Niven 83).

In the meantime promoter and abolitionist Eli Thayer had founded the Massachusetts Emigrant Aid Society, whose aim was to move New Englanders to the Kansas-Nebraska territories. The political implications of Thayer's business venture soon became obvious as proslavery and antislavery forces clashed violently, prompting the term "Bleeding Kansas." In this context, Charles Sumner in May 1856 stood in the Senate to deliver his speech "The Crime against Kansas."

The "crime" Sumner describes metaphorically as the "rape of a virgin territory, compelling it to the hateful embrace of slavery." It is the result of a "depraved longing for a new slave state, the hideous offspring of such a crime" (Sumner 5). The criminal Sumner refers to by the epithet "Slave Power," an abolitionist term appropriated by other Northerners who promoted "free" labor. Underlying the term "Slave Power" was the belief that it was a conspiratorial force controlling the federal government (Foner 9). By describing recent events in Kansas as rape and the Slave Power as rapist, Sumner exceeded the bounds of senatorial convention and taste. Further, he included *ad hominem* attacks on both Senator Douglas and South Carolina senator Andrew Butler, who occupied the seat next to Sumner but was absent during his speech. Comparing them to Don Quixote and Sancho Panza, Sumner sneered that though Butler "believes himself a chivalrous knight," he has chosen the "harlot Slavery" as his mistress, who "though ugly to others is always lovely to him; though polluted in the sight of the world, is chaste in his sight" (9).

Senators who heard Sumner's speech and many other people who read about it in newspapers were troubled by Sumner's vitriolic diatribe against the elderly South Carolina senator. Edward Everett, who was then the other senator from Massachusetts, commented in his diary, "Language equally intemperate and bitter is sometimes heard from a notorious parliamentary blackguard, but from a man of character of any party I have never seen anything so offensive" (qtd. in Donald 288). In Everett's estimation, Sumner had exceeded the bounds of propriety by using insulting and offensive language no "man of character" would use.

While Everett could record his regrets privately, Southerners brought up under the "code of honor" interpreted Sumner's remarks as so deeply insulting that they required public retribution. To Congressman Preston Brooks, a cousin of Senator Butler, the obvious public acknowledgment of insult would be to challenge Sumner to a duel. He did not take this course of action, however, for two reasons. First, he surmised that the "moral tone of mind that would lead a man to come a Black Republican would make him incapable of courage" (qtd. in Donald 291). In other words, Brooks believed that Sumner would not accept his challenge. Second, according to the code, a duel was between social equals, and Brooks did not consider Sumner his equal. In that case, according to the code, one used a "cane or horsewhip" on the offender (Donald 291). Because Sumner was bigger and stronger, Brooks chose as his weapon a cane with a gold head. Two days after Sumner's speech, he attacked Sumner at his seat on the Senate floor, pounding his head until Sumner fell bleeding and unconscious. Brooks instantly rose to heroic stature in the South, and a Senate committee investigating the incident reported that since Brooks was a member of the House, the incident was outside the Senate's jurisdiction (Donald 298).

In New England, however, the story was different. New Englanders were outraged that one of their own had been beaten in the hallowed halls of the Senate and by a Southerner. Sumner became an instant martyr for the abolitionist cause. That he had conducted himself in an ungentlemanly fashion by using aggressive and combative rhetoric was ignored and forgotten as the New England intelligentsia became more disposed to military action against the South. At a meeting in Concord, Emerson described Sumner as having the "whitest soul I ever knew" and declared that because of the incident every sane human being had become an abolitionist (*Anti-Slavery Writings* 109). Where before Emerson had equated abolitionism with fanaticism and odiousness, now he equated it with purity and sanity.

At Sumner's death in 1874, Higginson eulogized him by recalling his 1845 Fourth of July Oration. He remembered a prominent merchant remarking, "Well, if that young man is going to talk in that way, he cannot expect Boston to hold him up." Higginson writes that though Boston at first did not hold Sumner up, "Massachusetts so sustained him that he held up Boston, until it had learned to sustain him in return" (*Contemporaries* 281). Though Sumner's violent words had degraded him, Preston Brooks's cane succeeded in elevating him to heroic stature.

After the caning of Sumner, which the North considered a barbarous act, the great differences between the North and South could no longer be ignored. Stating the New England position, Emerson remarked that a civilized community and a barbarous community cannot exist as a union. "In one, it is adorned with education, with skilful labor, with arts, with long prospective interests, with sacred family ties, with honor and justice. In the other, life is a fever; man is an animal, given to pleasure, frivolous, irritable, spending his days on hunting and practising with deadly weapons to defend himself against his slaves, and against his companions brought up in the same idle and dangerous way. Such people live for the moment, they have properly no future, and readily risk on every passion a life which is of small value to themselves or to others" (*Anti-Slavery Writings* 107). Emerson reiterates the old split between reason and passion that was so prominent in the philosophy of the Scottish Enlightenment. The North represented reason, the South passion. Conceiving Sumner as a New England martyr for the cause of civilization and morality enabled Emerson and others to maintain their conception of all Southerners as passionate, uncivilized, and immoral enemies of rational progress.

In his articles in *The Liberator*, William Lloyd Garrison had long been arguing that the South presented a threat to New England culture. For Garrison, mere association with slavery made all Southerners guilty and evil, and abolishing slavery was the only means of redemption. After abolition/redemption, the South would become a place of perfect harmony. Using the imagery and balance of biblical rhetoric, Garrison writes in the voice of God: "Instead of darkness, you shall have light; instead of tribulation, joy; instead of adversity, prosperity. For barrenness, you shall have fertility; for wasteful, indolent and revengeful serfs, provident, industrious, and grateful laborers; for liability to servile insurrections, perfect exemption from danger. The execrations of your victims shall be turned into blessings; their wailings into shouts of joy; the judgments of God into mercies. Your peace shall flow like a river, for there shall be none to molest or make afraid" (qtd. in Floan 6).

Once slavery is conceived in religious terms as a sin, then abolition must be conceived in terms of redemption and salvation. But biblical rhetoric can go no further. As Sallie McFague notes in *Metaphorical Theology,* religious language without religious context becomes both idolatrous and irrelevant, idolatrous because it absolutizes and irrelevant because it excludes all other ways of reasoning (13). I would add that another problem with using religious rhetoric to talk about slavery and abolition is that, as Garrison has so aptly demonstrated, the end of religious rhetoric is salvation. If slaveowners are sinners, abolition is redemption, and post-abolition is salvation. There simply is nowhere to go after salvation. Garrison's religious rhetoric that saves the sinners from the sin of slavery ends with Southern slaveholders freeing slaves and thus ignores the need for any other human agency. Containing no elements of deliberation, Garrison's rhetoric, like Sumner's, is exhortative and absolute, grounded in universal religious principles that enable both men to speak and write without having to deal with difficult issues. They merely proclaim, and their proclamations are sanctioned by God.

By the time the Confederates attacked Fort Sumter in 1861, New England had not one martyr but two—Charles Sumner and John Brown. John Brown became famous in New England as an antislavery soldier in Kansas. Higginson, who had been to Kansas and heard about Brown, praised him in 1857 at a meeting of the Massachusetts Anti-Slavery Society: "Old Captain Brown, the Ethan Allen, the Israel Putnam of today, who has prayers every morning, and then sallies forth, with seven stalwart sons, wherever duty or danger calls, who swallows a Missourian whole, and says grace after the meat" (qtd. in Edelstein 196).

While Higginson praised Brown, he remained silent on Brown's legendary bloody escapade. After proslavery Missourians had raided Lawrence, Kansas, Brown had retaliated by leading a group of armed men across the Pottawatomie Creek and butchering five unarmed Missouri settlers. From the very beginning of their relationship with Brown, New England abolitionists and Kansas Relief advocates ignored Brown's violent fanaticism.

In 1857 Franklin Sanborn, Emerson's neighbor in Concord and secretary of the Massachusetts Free Soil party, brought Brown to Concord to deliver a speech and raise money with which to purchase arms. While in Concord, Brown lunched with the Thoreaus and spent a night with the Emersons. John Brown returned to Concord in May of 1859 in another effort to raise money for his cause. Again Emerson and Thoreau heard him speak. Five days later, Brown and eighteen followers attacked the Federal arsenal at Harper's Ferry, Virginia. They were arrested and charged with treason. Writing to his brother William about the event, Emerson described Brown as "a true hero" but admitted that Brown had "lost his head" (qtd. in Gougeon 238).

Implicated with Brown's raid on Harper's Ferry were six supporters called the "Secret Six": Gerrit Smith, Samuel Gridley Howe, George Stearns, Theodore Parker, Franklin Sanborn, and Thomas Wentworth Higginson. After Brown's capture, Howe, Stearns, and Sanborn fled immediately to Canada, Parker was already out of the country, and Smith had himself confined to the New York State Asylum for the Insane. Only Higginson remained, but he was never arrested, nor was he called to testify before the Senate Investigating Committee. Higginson believed he was not called because congressmen, when "white men are concerned . . . will yield before the slightest resistance" (qtd. in Edelstein 233).

After the raid but before Brown's execution, Emerson spoke about Brown at a meeting to raise money for his family. Predicting that Brown would be famous in history, Emerson said, "Nothing can resist the sympathy which all elevated minds must feel with Brown, and through them the whole civilized world." He praised Brown as an idealist who did not rely on "moral suasion" but rather put his ideals into action. Emerson argued, "He saw how deceptive the forms are. We fancy, in Massachusetts, that we are free; yet it seems the Government is quite unreliable. Great wealth,—great population,—men of talent in the executive, on the Bench,—all the forms right,—and yet, life and freedom are not safe. Why? Because the judges rely on the forms, and do not, like John Brown, use their eyes to see the fact behind the forms" (*Anti-Slavery Writings* 118–19).

Emerson uses the metaphors of form and fact to differentiate laws and institutions from the human experience of their effects. In a later speech before the Massachusetts Anti-Slavery Society, a speech interrupted by hecklers, Emerson argues that the institution of slavery "seems to stupify the moral sense" and subvert reason (*Anti-Slavery Writings* 126). Keeping intact the moral sense and reason, Emerson implies, requires concrete action, such as that of John Brown. But Emerson, arguing that "elevated minds" and the "civilized world" are in "sympathy" with Brown, ignores the violence of Brown's action.

After the caning of Sumner, Emerson's public statements reveal a gradual revision of the role of the intellectual in abolishing slavery. When, in late 1856, the *Boston Advertiser* reported that Oliver Wendell Holmes denounced New England abolitionists as "traitors to the Union," Emerson admonished Holmes in a letter. He wrote that though a "scholar need not be cynical to feel that the vast multitude are almost on all fours," yet the "pathetically small minority of disengaged or thinking men [must] stand for the ideal right, for man as he should be" (qtd. in Gougeon 219). This statement reveals Emerson's rhetorical skill as he deals with the vanity of Holmes. Placing himself and Holmes within the "pathetically small minority," Emerson argues that intellectuals must tell the animalistic "vast multitude" what and how to think. Since to Emerson the "ideal right" means moral principles, the "thinking" man can argue in abstract terms and thus remain "disengaged." Unlike John Brown, who saw the "fact behind the form" and acted on what he saw, the scholar remains on his pedestal, the writer hidden behind his pen. Nevertheless, despite Emerson's vacillation between engagement and detachment in the abolition movement, when federal marshals came to Concord to take Franklin Sanborn, who was under subpoena by the Senate committee investigating Harper's Ferry, Emerson was in the citizen's group that stood between the marshals and Sanborn and prevented his arrest.

After Brown's conviction, Higginson, who had more reason than Emerson to see Brown martyred, confided to his mother, "I don't feel sure that his acquittal or rescue would do half as much good as being executed" (qtd. in Edelstein 225). Later he changed his mind and traveled to Brown's home on a mission to have Mary, John Brown's wife, convince her husband that a rescue was desirable. Brown protested that he did not want his wife to visit nor did he desire to be rescued. Mrs. Brown did visit, however, and an elaborate rescue plan was laid, but the attempt never materialized and Brown was executed.

Immediately after Brown's execution, James Redpath published a book entitled *The Public Life of John Brown.* Redpath, however, fails to mention Brown in Kansas since, as he told Higginson, it "degrades him from the position of a Puritan 'warring of the Lord' to a guerrilla chief of vindictive character" (qtd. in Edelstein 231). Included in the book is Higginson's account of his visit to the Brown household ("A Visit to John Brown's Household in 1859" reprinted in *Contemporaries* 219–43).

Silent about the real reason for his visit, Higginson frames his article as a journey. The story thus is coded as a travel story: the difficult journey, the arrival, the description of the house and farm, the pause at the threshold, the cataloguing of what the traveler hears and sees inside the household, the summing up of what the traveler learns, and the journey back.

The traveler, whose task is to observe the environment and its inhabitants, is being observed and interpolated by the writer. As the traveler enters the "enchanted land" and selects the "least frequented" and "most difficult" route, he is confronted with a "wall of mountain" and a "wild gap" that he must penetrate. The passageway, or "cave of iron," winding through woods and over a steep mountain precipice, figures as the traveler's test of courage.

Upon the traveler's arrival, he sees a "little frame house, unpainted," surrounded by black stumps, and more widely surrounded by "heaven." His eyes fall upon an "old, mossy, time-worn tombstone" that rests against the house "as if its time were either past or not yet come." The tombstone is inscribed with two names: Captain John Brown, Revolutionary War soldier, and Frederick Brown, "murdered at Osawatomie for his adherence to the cause of freedom." Together the house and the tombstone figure as endurance and inevitability. As the traveler pauses to "raise the latch of this humble door," his steps falter, and the writer intrudes to tell the reader that his pen falters also. The traveler will enter; the writer will construe meaning. "This home is a home of sacred sorrow," Higginson writes. "How shall we enter it?" He answers, "Do not shrink; you are not near the world; you are near John Brown's household." Sacralizing Brown's house and household establishes the interpretative mode the writer will use to impose meaning upon the traveler's observations.

He observes the members of the household: Mrs. Brown, a young son and his wife, the widows of two slain sons, and three young daughters. Family members bring out letters, books, and daguerreotypes, until "at last the rosy little Ellen brought me, with reverent hands, her prime treasure"—a Bible given to her and inscribed by her father. The inscription admonishes her that the Bible "is not intended for common use, but to be carefully preserved for her and by her, in remembrance of her father." Mrs. Brown, the "sharer of [Brown's] plans," relates that she and her husband had always believed that "he was to be an instrument in the hands of Providence." Other members of the Brown household people the story only for the benefit of the traveler and the writer. For the traveler, they are John Brown's messengers and bearers of marvelous items. For the writer, they become enabling shadow figures—the writer selects from what they bring and what they say in order to construct John Brown as martyr.

Mrs. Brown's statement that she does not care to attend church services where slavery is not mentioned and Ellen's bringing the Bible to the traveler prompt the writer to construct John Brown as Puritan, both in "theology" and in "practice," a devout man whose singular mission was liberating slaves. Brown, the writer argues, was not a "vindictive guerrilla, nor a maddened Indian." He was rather a visionary who "saw at a glance . . . what the rest of us are only beginning to see, even now—that slavery must be met, first or last, on its own ground."

Higginson compares knowing the Browns to a "liberal education." "Lord Byron," he writes, "could not help clinging to Shelley, because he said he was the only person in whom he saw anything like disinterested benevolence." But Byron, Higginson argues, "might well have exchanged his wealth, his peerage, and his genius" for a brief training with the Browns. The writer's allusion to Byron and Shelley, out of place within the Brown household, reminds the reader that the traveler/writer belongs in a different world, a literary realm. Soon the traveler takes his leave, going "down from the mountains, and out through the iron gorge," leaving "wiser and better." Given Higginson's involvement in Brown's clandestine activities, he had to construct Brown as Puritan hero in order to justify his own actions. By sacralizing Brown's farm, his house, and his family, Higginson succeeds in mythicizing Brown as hero.

James Russell Lowell's shifting sentiments about war matched his changing attitudes about slavery. Concerning the Mexican War (1846–1848), he had written in the voice of Ezekial Biglow:

> Ez fer war, I call it murder,—
> There you hev it plain an' flat;
> I don't want to go no furder
> Than my Testyment fer that.
> ("The Biglow Papers No. 1" in *Poetical Works* 181)

Lowell perceived the Mexican War as a triumph for the South, whose aim had been to annex Texas as a slave state and thereby to gain more power for the institution of slavery. The North, he believed, had been duped into fighting the war. At the end of the poem, Lowell has Ezekial suggest dissolving the Union:

> Ef I'd *my* way I hed ruther
> We should go to work an' part,
> They take one way, we take t'other,
> Guess it would n't break my heart;
> Man hed ought' to put asunder
> Them thet God has noways jined;
> An' I should n't gretly wonder
> Ef there's thousands o' my mind.
> (*Poetical Works* 183)

Abolitionists had been divided upon the issue of disunion. Garrison and Wendell Phillips had long favored separation, believing that once the South was left to its own resources, the institution of slavery would some-

how dissolve. Phillips argued, "If lawful and peaceful efforts for the abolition of slavery in our land will dissolve it, let the Union go . . . perish the
Union, when its cement must be the blood of the slave" (qtd. in Bartlett
66).

In an 1860 lecture, Emerson suggested that disunion would be a triumph for radical individualism. The time had come, he argued, to abandon "much of the machinery of government" and leave "to every man all
his rights and powers, checked by no law but his love or fear of the rights
and powers of his neighbor" (qtd. in Fredrickson, *Inner Civil War* 54). In
his attempted speech at Boston's Tremont Temple in 1861, Emerson said
that the bond between the North and South had ceased to exist. They
were separated "in sympathy, in thought, in character." What, then, he
asked, is the use of a "pretended tie?" (*Anti-Slavery Writings* 127).

In 1857, Higginson called for a Massachusetts Disunion Convention,
which convened in Worcester. Arguing against the pacifism Garrison advocated, Higginson supported militant action. The time for political agi-
tation, he believed, had passed: "Give me a convention of ten who have
drawn the sword for right, and *thrown away the scabbard,* and I will revo-
lutionize the world" (qtd. in Edelstein 199). This statement signals the
completion of Higginson's move from social reformer to "revolutionist."
Given his increasing militancy, it is little wonder that Higginson supported John Brown.

Wendell Phillips, however, aligning himself with Garrisonian reform
and redemption, still believed in the power of rhetoric. He argued that
first the word "disunion" needed to become familiar to the "public ear";
then "leave events to stereotype it into practice" (Edelstein 200). Phillips
would have understood "stereotype" as the process in printing of mold-
ing a cast in type metal. "Stereotyping disunion into practice" thus meant
that first the concept becomes a set form, then the form becomes interpolated as action. Such a process, Phillips understood, takes time. As Northern conceptions of Southerners had to evolve over time—from thinking
human beings to uncivilized and barbarous animals—so the idea of disunion had to evolve, first as word, then as concept, and finally as action.
Furthermore, leaving "events to stereotype [disunion] into practice"
erases human agency and responsibility. Phillips implies that if "events"
become violent, somebody else commits the violence. The speaker or
writer whose words have incited the violent action remains detached and
disinterested, that is, clean and safe.

By 1860 disunion was imminent. By February 1861, seven Southern
states had seceded and established a Provisional Confederacy with Jefferson Davis as president. In April, the Confederates attacked and captured
Fort Sumter, a Federal fort in Charleston Harbor. The war had begun. In
an article entitled "E Pluribus Unum" published in the *Atlantic* in Febru-

ary 1861, James Russell Lowell no longer called war "murder" nor argued for peaceful disunion. Now he redefined terms: "The country is weary of being cheated with plays upon words. . . . Rebellion smells no sweeter because it is called Secession, nor does Order lose its divine precedence in human affairs because a knave may nickname it Coercion. Secession means chaos, and Coercion the exercise of legitimate authority" (*Political Essays* 65–66).

To the South's contention that states had entered the Union voluntarily and therefore had the right to secede, Lowell countered, "The United States are not a German Confederation, but a unitary and indivisible nation, with a national life to protect, a national power to maintain, and national rights to defend against any and every assailant, at all hazards. Our national existence is all that gives value to American citizenship" (*Political Essays* 61). If, as Lowell argued, the Union is "unitary and indivisible," then "coercion" is not "violence, but merely the assertion of constituted and acknowledged authority" (*Political Essays* 83).

Lowell begins by protesting "plays on words," but demonstrates throughout the article that he also can play with words, and further, that he understands the significance of word play. Thus "secession" is "rebellion" and "chaos," and seceders are not "discontented citizens" but rather "open rebels with arms in their hands" (*Political Essays* 78). "Coercion" is neither force nor "violence," but instead the assertion of national authority. National authority, Lowell indicates, is the only "legitimate" authority. Lowell's arguments and definitions legitimize the power of the Union and validate his own self-constitution as subject allied to the nation and thus fortified against the disorder and danger of chaotic rebellion.

In his article "Bread and Newspapers" published in the *Atlantic* in September 1861, Oliver Wendell Holmes uses a different strategy to fortify himself. Usually silent on slavery and abolition, Holmes suddenly becomes vocal as an ardent Unionist. He contends, "War has taught us, as nothing else could, what we can be and are." Even our "poor New England Brahmins" who are "commonly pallid, undervitalized, shy, sensitive creatures, whose only birthright is an aptitude for learning" are becoming men whose "courage is big enough for the uniform which hangs so loosely about their slender figures" (*Pages* 8–9).

Holmes's perception of war as bringing to the surface men's noble qualities and his ardent Unionist rhetoric were prompted by the enlistment of his son Oliver Wendell Holmes, Jr. In trouble at Harvard for insulting faculty members and breaking windows, Wendell enlisted as a private, leaving Harvard two months before graduation. After completing his training, however, instead of being sent to battle, he was returned home where he finished the academic year at Harvard but was denied a part in commencement exercises. After Wendell was unsuccessful in being granted an officer's commission, Dr. Holmes began to pull strings, finally visiting the governor. As a result, Private Oliver Wendell Holmes, Jr., became Lieutenant Holmes and later Captain Holmes. And the war became for his father "our Holy War," fought between the forces of God and the forces of Satan.

Though Holmes had disparaged Calvinism all his adult life, now he spoke and wrote with the voice of a Calvinist preacher: "This is our Holy War, and we must fight it against that great General who will bring to it all the powers with which he fought against the Almighty before he was cast down from heaven. He has retained many a cunning advocate to recruit for him; he has bribed many a smooth-tongued preacher to be his chaplain; he has engaged the sordid by their avarice, the timid by their fears, the profligate by their love of adventure, and thousands of nobler natures by motives which we can all understand; whose delusion we pity as we ought always to pity the error of those who know not what they do" (*Pages* 117). The trope of "God's kingdom," the description of the cunning operations of evil, the images, the repetition, and the cadence are that of the old-time Calvinist preacher. War apparently had taken away Dr. Holmes's belief in science, progress, and literature, and returned him to the religion of his father.

Envisioning the war as advancing God's kingdom on earth, Holmes imagines at the end of the war, on the "day of deliverance," there will be multitudes of "white Southerners" who will welcome Northerners. At that point the North will "overrun and by degrees . . . recolonize the South." This process "may be a part of the mechanism of its new birth, spreading from various centres of organization, on the plan which Nature follows when she would fill a half-finished tissue with blood-vessels or change a temporary cartilage into bone" (*Pages* 103). Here Holmes introduces a new element—the North recolonizing the South—and suggests that recolonization will be organized according to natural/divine law. If New Englanders could not spread their high culture by "elevation" and education, they could just move South.

In a similar vein, Lowell had argued that the laws of "every human government" reflect God's laws. That is, they are "uniform, certain, and unquestionable in their operation" and therefore carry the authority of "divine right inasmuch as its office is to maintain that order which is the single attribute of the Infinite Reason" (*Political Essays* 90). Because the law of the Union is God's law, the Union has established divine right, and Lowell imagines extending such a government until it becomes "a single empire embracing the whole world, and controlling, without extinguishing, local organizations and nationalities. . . . One language, one law, one citizenship over thousands of miles" (*Political Essays* 81). For Lowell and Holmes, "God's kingdom" has become Yankee Empire.

In *Culture and Imperialism*, Edward Said notes that many British Victorian writers imagined an "international display of British power virtually unchecked over the entire world." It was logical and easy for them to identify with empire because of the way they wrote about British culture, morality, taste, and education. Said contends that to represent these subjects, to influence and mold them rhetorically, was also to perceive them globally (105). Similarly, Benedict Anderson argues in *Imagined Communities* that print technology shaped one group's experience into a unity, creating the experience as a thing: a concept, a model, a blueprint, a nation (80–81). The New England writers I have been discussing perhaps did not imagine empire exactly as the British Victorians, but as the writing of Lowell and Holmes indicates, they imagined a Yankee empire. They wrote about it, created it as a possibility, and saw the war as their opportunity to build it.

Not only had Lowell and Holmes molded and shaped ideas about New England high culture based on morality and taste, but they also had written the war as a holy war whose outcome would decide whether the New England version of culture and morality could continue its existence. To exist at all, they recognized, New England culture had to be extended to the South. Therefore, just as New England had sent emigrants to Kansas to fight against the extension of slavery there, it would send emigrants to the South to recolonize, to become the "mechanism for new birth," and to spread the gospel of New England culture. Equally as important, the emigrants would organize the South according to rationality, uniformity, and certainty. Representing God as "Infinite Reason" enables Lowell to envision an embracing and controlling empire founded on reason and order.

Furthermore, in juxtaposing "embracing" and "controlling" Lowell marks the connection between desire and control. When desire becomes the drive to produce (the "desiring machine" of Deleuze and Guattari), then "producing," "embracing," and "controlling" lose their distinctions; or, as Deleuze and Guattari put it, "desire clasps life in its powerfully productive embrace and reproduces it" (27). As a product of a desiring machine, the act of writing produces, embraces, and controls. In "The Idea of Order at Key West," the poet Wallace Stevens named this phenomenon, which writers know only too well, the "blessed rage for order." As writers, Lowell and Holmes responded to the destruction and violence of war by producing/writing a South embraced and controlled by a New England Empire of God/Reason.

Where Lowell and Holmes became desiring machines and superpatriots for God and Union, for Higginson the war figured differently. In 1870 in a book entitled *Army Life in a Black Regiment,* Higginson published his war experiences, the story of his service as colonel of the First South Carolina Volunteers, the first regiment of ex-slaves in the Union army. Stationed near Beaufort, South Carolina, for two years Higginson and his regiment of black soldiers explored and invaded the coastal and island regions of South Carolina, Georgia, and northern Florida. In discussing *Army Life,* I am bracketing the extent to which Higginson told the "truth" about events. Both Leon Edelstein in *Strange Enthusiasm* and Edmund Wilson in *Patriotic Gore* have pointed out the disparity between the accounts in *Army Life* and other accounts of events, including Higginson's own journal entries. *Army Life* is not so much a memoir of the Civil War— there is almost no violence—as a story of Higginson's ambiguous enthrallment with the South and with the black soldiers.

Higginson writes that when General Rufus Saxton offered him the command, he was reluctant to accept, but "it took but a few days in South Carolina to make it clear that all was right." In this passage Higginson's "it," which replaces a subject, leaves the reader wondering about agency. In the last sentence in the paragraph, Higginson attempts to explain his decision to accept the command: "I had been an abolitionist too long, and had known and loved John Brown too well, not to feel a thrill of joy at last on finding myself in the position where he only wished to be" (*Army Life* 3). Higginson implies that by commanding the black troops he is a kind of substitute for John Brown. Yet Higginson knew that Brown was neither disciplined enough nor aristocratic enough to be a colonel. One reason for Higginson's decision might be that he knew he would be immediately thrust into the national limelight. As he notes, his battalion of black soldiers created quite a "spectacle"; they were watched "with microscopic scrutiny by friends and foes" (4).

As Higginson describes in his diary his trip to camp, he seems propelled by external forces: "Steaming over the summer sea," "no land in sight, no sail." The sun, providing the only illumination, submerged "in one vast bank of rosy suffusion" and darkness fell; "then the moon set, a moon two days old, a curved pencil of light, reclining backwards on a radiant couch which seem to rise from the waves to receive it." In the morning "Hilton Head lay on one side, the gunboats on the other; all that was raw and bare in the low buildings of the new settlement was softened into picturesqueness by the early light" (5). Higginson's romantic imagery, making it difficult for the reader to remember that he is going to war, indicates a certain driftedness, a willingness to be seduced by what he sees and imagines.

At first Higginson tries to compare the landscape to that of New England: "The shores were low and wooded, like any New England shore" (5).

Later, he concedes that the "chilly sunshine and the pale blue river seem like New England, but those alone." At this point, New England fades into distant memory. Here I will record at length an entry from his camp diary made four days after his arrival:

> The air is full of noisy drumming, and of gunshots; for the prize-shooting is our great celebration of the day, and the drumming is chronic. My young barbarians are all at play. I look out from the broken windows of this forlorn plantation-house, through avenues of great live-oaks, with their hard, shining leaves, and their branches hung with a universal drapery of soft, long moss, like fringe-trees struck with grayness. Below, the sandy soil, scantily covered with coarse grass, bristles with sharp palmettos and aloes; all the vegetation is stiff, shining, semi-tropical, with nothing soft or delicate in its texture. Numerous plantation-buildings totter around, all slovenly and unattractive, while the interspaces are filled with all manner of wreck and refuse, pigs, fowls, dogs, and omnipresent Ethiopian infancy. All this is the universal Southern panorama; but five minutes' walk beyond the hovels and the live-oaks will bring one to something so un-Southern that the whole Southern coast at this moment trembles at the suggestion of such a thing—the camp of a regiment of free slaves. (7)

Higginson's command requires that he transform this "regiment of freed slaves" into soldiers, a task that requires order, discipline, and disinterestedness, all those inbred and cultivated New England characteristics. In light of his enormous task, one might expect that Higginson's writing would reflect these same characteristics as well as high moral absoluteness. Instead of Lowell's and Holmes's rage for order, however, Higginson's writing reveals an increasing awareness that the "Southern panorama," the "drumming," the "wreck and refuge," the "Ethiopian"-ness, and the "gunshots" might not yield themselves easily to New England ideas of order, nor does the writer seem to want them to. If the reader begins to think that Higginson might be experiencing a crisis of certainty, the paragraph that follows supplies confirmation: "Already I am growing used to the experience, at first so novel, of living among five hundred men, and scarce a white face to be seen,—of seeing them go through all their daily processes, eating, frolicking, talking, just as if they were white. Each day at dress-parade I stand with the customary folding of the arms before a regimental line of countenances so black that I can hardly tell whether the men stand steadily or not; black is every hand which moves in ready cadence as I vociferate, 'Battalion! Shoulder arms!' nor is it till the line of white officers moves forward, as parade is dismissed, that I am reminded that my own face is not the color of coal" (7).

At their leisure, the ex-slaves eat, frolic, and talk "just as if they were white," and at parade they respond as disciplined soldiers (just as if they were white soldiers). During the first months, the black soldiers become whiter to Higginson, though never entirely white, and he becomes, in his own perception, black. The only real white men are the white officers, who in this passage as well as in most of the book, are effaced of their individuality, written as a "line of white officers." The world Higginson writes comprises only the white-black Higginson and his black-white barbarians-cum-soldiers.

Yet since, as Higginson admits, he has had "little personal intercourse with the men," they concern him "chiefly in bulk as so many consumers of rations, wearers of uniform, bearers of muskets. But as the machine comes into shape, I am beginning to decipher the individual parts." Deciphering the individual parts consists in noticing color gradations, so that men from Florida, he notices, are lighter in complexion and "look more intelligent" (7–8).

From Thanksgiving to New Year's Day, Higginson relates three episodes that figure significantly in his chronicle. The first takes place one evening as he was "strolling in the moonlight" and "was attracted by a brilliant light." Approaching it, he finds thirty or forty men sitting around a fire listening to an old man tell a story. The story, which Higginson records in vernacular dialect, has several subplots in which the speaker, elaborating on what he knows about the territory and about white people, manages finally to escape to a Union vessel. By feigning humility, fright, and ignorance, he manages to extract information, obtain food, and flag down a passing Union boat. Higginson genuinely is captivated with the storyteller, the story, the listeners, their responses, and the magical setting: "Overhead, the mighty limbs of a great live-oak, with the weird moss swaying in the smoke, and the high moon gleaming faintly through." Higginson concludes, "This is their university; every young Sambo before me, as he turned over the sweet potatoes and peanuts which were roasting in the ashes, listened with reverence to the wiles of the ancient Ulysses, and meditated the same. It is Nature's compensation: oppression simply crushes the upper faculties of the head, and crowds everything into the perceptive organs" (9–11).

The second event is a "shout" which Higginson describes as "that strange festival, half pow-wow, half prayer-meeting." "Shouts" take place in an enclosure of palm leaves, a "regular native African hut," with a fire in the middle. The men begin to sing "in one of their quaint, monotonous, endless, negro-Methodist chants, with obscure syllables recurring constantly, and slight variations interwoven, all accompanied with a regular drumming of the feet and clapping of the hands, like castanets." Then as the excitement spreads, the men begin to dance. Some of the dancers heel and toe, "others merely tremble and stagger on, others stoop and rise, others whirl, others caper sideways, all keep steadily circling like dervishes," until finally "there comes a sort of snap, and the spell breaks, amid general sighing and laughter. And this not rarely and occasionally, but night after night, while in other parts of the camp the soberest prayers and exhortations are proceeding sedately" (13–14).

The third event occurs on New Year's Day at the formal ceremony accompanying the reading of the Emancipation Proclamation. Higginson writes that the service began at half past eleven with prayer, followed by the reading of the Proclamation, then the presentation of the colors. "All this was according to the programme." The moment he takes the flag, "there suddenly arose, close beside the platform, a strong male voice, (but rather cracked and elderly), into which two women's voices instantly blended, singing, as if by an impulse that could no more be repressed than the morning note of the song-sparrow.—'My Country, 'tis of thee, Sweet land of liberty, Of thee I sing.'" Higginson writes, "People looked at each other, and then at us on the platform, to see whence came this interruption, not set down in the bills." But the "quavering voices sang on, verse after verse." Other blacks joined in, but when whites on the platform began to sing, Higginson motions them to silence. "I never saw anything so electric," he writes. "It made all other words cheap" (30–31).

At the same time that Higginson is fascinated with the splendid novelty of the black soldiers, he is obsessed with uniformity. One morning as he happens upon a review and drill of white regiments in Beaufort, he notes the "absence of uniformity in minor points" and notes that the "prescribed 'Tactics' approach perfection; it is never left discretionary in what place an officer shall stand, or in what words he shall give his order. All variation would seem to imply negligence." The small points, he argues, "are not merely a matter of punctilio; for the more perfectly a battalion is drilled on the parade-ground, the more quietly it can be handled in action." Because on a battlefield soldiers of different companies might be intermingled, a "diversity of orders may throw everything into confusion." From the specifics of drilling, Higginson moves to "handling a regiment" then to "governing." He concludes that "it is as easy to govern a regiment as a school or a factory, and needs like qualities,—system, promptness, patience, tact" (34–35).

The first part of the book, taken from Higginson's journal entries, proceeds day by day/night by night and through a series of oppositions, some stated, some implied: New England/the South, black/white, night/day, novelty/uniformity, civilization/barbarism, order/disorder, maturity/childishness, Higginson the commander/Higginson the voyeur. As writer, Higginson sometimes narrates and describes and allows the words to stand for themselves without intruding, but at other times, attempting to impose order, he adds explanation.

The old "Ulysses" Higginson characterizes as a teacher, the "Sambos" as learners ("This is their university") who receive the lesson through their "perceptive organs," the "upper faculties" having been crushed by oppression. The "African" shout, primitive and wild, occurs "night after night" simultaneously with the sober and sedate prayer meeting. Higginson notes the formality and programmed agenda of the ceremony accompanying the reading of the Emancipation Proclamation. Yet the program is interrupted by the "quavering" but persevering voices of the black singers, and Higginson is so pleased with the performance that he motions the white people in the audience to remain silent.

The writer's rhetoric in these narratives exemplifies what Bakhtin calls "hybridization," and the Higginson inside the story, the written Higginson, becomes a hybrid. Bakhtin distinguishes between intentional and organic hybrids, and I would argue that Higginson's discourse embodies both. When he records the words of the black soldiers, he writes in the vernacular dialect, distinguishing their "primitive" and "childlike" language from his own "civilized" and "authoritative" language, the two languages representing two distinct consciousnesses or worldviews. Bakhtin calls this hybrid "intentional"; that is, Higginson the writer intends to indicate the distinctions, the separation, and he uses two languages to accomplish his rhetorical aim.

Organic hybridization, unintentional and unconscious, represents the merging of two individual consciousnesses (Bakhtin 358–60). I propose that Higginson, as he intentionally hybridizes his situation as white colonel commanding black soldiers, becomes organically hybridized, self-written as both white and black, primitive and civilized, Northern and Southern. Organic hybridization occurs as his roles shift back and forth from commander to voyeur. By day when he commands, he seeks uniformity, order, and reason. At night when he watches, listens, and desires, he seeks the disorder and wildness of Africa and the South, and the lessons he can learn by the "perceptive organs." When the "shout" occurs at the same time as the prayer meeting, Higginson is clear about which one he prefers to watch.

In contrast to the nighttime "shout," the Emancipation Proclamation ceremony is a daytime, formal, public occasion where Higginson must be commanding. The black singers inter-rupt the program without dis-rupting it, and Higginson takes charge by motioning the whites not to sing. Following his account of the incident, he elaborates by explaining its significance: "Just think of it!—the first day they had ever had a country, the first flag they had ever seen which promised anything to their people, and here, while mere spectators stood in silence, waiting for my stupid words, these simple souls burst out in their lay, as if they were by their own hearths at home! When they stopped, there was nothing to do for it but to speak, and I went on; but the life of the whole day was in those unknown people's song" (31). Here Higginson acknowledges and honors the singers and at the same time effaces them as "unknown people" and "simple souls" who act at a formal public ceremony as if they were at home. When he attempts self-effacement ("my stupid words"), the reader interprets it as mere display. There is no doubt about who commands the ceremony.

In his entry of 12 January, Higginson writes, "It was very dark the other night,—an unusual thing here,—and the rain fell in torrents; so I put on my India-rubber suit, and went the rounds of the sentinels, incognito, to test them." In this statement the "so" appears to mean "thus" or "therefore," as if putting on one's "India-rubber suit" naturally follows from darkness and torrential rain. In fact, Higginson puts on his India-rubber suit and pretends to be an intruder in order to test what he calls the "fidelity" of his sentinels. Here is Higginson disguising himself as black, putting on blackface, so to speak—or in this case, black-body—and playing the black trickster in order to test whether the soldiers on watch would allow him to pass without the "countersign."

Sometimes he refuses to give the password, sometimes he offers tobacco, sometimes he changes his voice—always with the same result. The sentinels will not let him pass. Finally, as it grows darker and rains harder, at the last watch, he gives the password: "Vicksburg." The sentinel, not understanding, answers, "Halt dar! Countersign nor correck." Higginson writes, "I tried persuasion, orthography, threats, tobacco, all in vain. I could not pass in. Of course my pride was up; for was I to defer to an untutored African on a point of pronunciation? Classic shades of Harvard, forbid! Affecting scornful indifference, I tried to edge away, proposing to myself to enter the camp at some other point, where my elocution would be better appreciated. Not a step could I stir." The guard holds Higginson at bayonet's edge until Higginson insists he call the corporal of the guard, at which time Higginson reveals himself, to the terror of the guard. Complimenting the guard on his fidelity, Higginson concludes that "the whole affair was very good for them all" (37–39).

In this scene Higginson is the intentional hybrid: he puts on his India-rubber suit, so he says, for a particular purpose—to administer the test. Although by wearing the suit he has made himself black, by writing the guard's words in dialect, he distinguishes his (white) language and, by extension, himself ("Classic shades of Harvard") from the guard. He prepares the reader for the guard's inability to understand the password by noting that "hard names" become "transformed upon their lips."

"Carthage" becomes "Cartridge" and "Concord" becomes "Corn-cob." Therefore, even though the guard literally holds Higginson prisoner, in the telling of this narrative, as in the narrative about the Emancipation Proclamation ceremony, Higginson the commander is inside the scene, though this time incognito, as Higginson the writer directs and organizes the scene.

Higginson writes another scene, however, that casts significance upon his role shift between commander and voyeur. Higginson and his regiment have moved to Port Royal, an island off the coast of South Carolina, not far from Charleston, where they are assigned picket duty to protect a seven-mile shoreline along the Coosaw River, with the Rebel pickets nearby on the South Carolina mainland across the causeway. Higginson comments, "To those doing outpost-duty on an island, however large, the main-land has all the fascination of forbidden fruit, and on a scale bounded only by the horizon. . . . Every grove in that blue distance appears enchanted ground, and yonder loitering gray-back leading his horse to water in the farthest distance, makes one thrill with a desire to hail him, to shoot at him, to capture him, to do anything to bridge this inexorable dumb space that lies between" (115). Again, it is night, and Higginson remarks that the "excitements of war are quadrupled by darkness; and as I rode along our outer lines at night, and watched the glimmering flames which at regular intervals starred the opposite river-shore, the longing was irresistible to cross the barrier of dusk, and see whether it were men or ghosts who hovered round those dying embers" (116). Higginson, the voyeur, apparently is going to try to taste the forbidden fruit.

Walking down the path to the river, past "my men" who resembled "black statues," he hands the lieutenant his watch and tells him he is going to take a swim. Stripping off his clothes and slipping "noiselessly into the placid water," he experiences a great sense of exhilaration. "The night was so still and lovely, my black statues looked so dream-like at their posts behind the low earthwork, the opposite arm of the causeway stretched so invitingly from the Rebel main, the horizon glimmered so low around me . . . that I seemed floating in some concave globe, some magic crystal, of which I was the enchanted centre" (118). After swimming for about a mile, he approaches the other side where he stays for awhile, watching the "dim figures of men moving to and fro upon the end of the causeway" (120).

Arousing a dog who starts to bark, Higginson decides he has seen enough and sinks below the surface, swimming as far as he can underwater toward his home shore. When he emerges finally, he realizes he is lost, and for a minute fears that he might be heading back toward the Rebel shore. Looking at the stars, he realizes that he is swimming in the right direction, but that he is nowhere near the place from which he started.

Now, "with some sense of fatigue," he finds it difficult to keep his "faith steady and [his] progress true; everything appeared to shift and waver" (121). Now he begins "to doubt everything, to distrust the stars, the line of low bushes for which I was wearily striving, the very land on which they grew. . . . Doubts trembled in my mind like the weltering water." He is "absorbed in that singular sensation of nightmare" and begins to believe that a man "might lose all power of direction, and so move in an endless circle until he sank exhausted. . . . It was as if a fissure opened somewhere, and I saw my way into a mad-house; then it closed, and everything went on as before." He decides that "imagination had no business here. That way madness lay. There was shore somewhere before me, and I must get to it, by the ordinary means. . . . That was all" (122–23).

Higginson makes it to shore, though nowhere near his clothes, climbs out of the water, presents himself naked to the sentinel—"the unconscionable fellow, wishing to exhaust upon me the utmost resources of military hospitality, deliberately presented arms!" (124). Finding his way to a building and procuring a blanket, he sits before a fire until "horse and clothing could be brought around," then mounts his horse and gallops home, falls immediately to sleep, and wakes a "few hours after in excellent condition" (125).

I read this fictionalized narrative as Higginson's crisis of faith in the Union cause in general, in the ability to endure his situation as commander of ex-slaves, and in his ability to hold together the hybrid he has become. In the narrative the space ("the inexorable dumb space") between North and South becomes narrowed to a mile of water between island and mainland, a distance Higginson is certain he is capable of bridging. On the other side, the Rebel side, lies the Garden of Eden metonymized as "forbidden fruit." Once Higginson decides to plunge in and close the "dumb space," he becomes the "enchanted centre" of a magic crystal. When he reaches the other side, however, the magic disappears as the barking dog and his own recollections of ex-slaves' stories about the viciousness of plantation dogs bring him back to reality.

Higginson has allowed his voyeuristic tendencies to lead him into an extremely dangerous situation, and he therefore decides to return expeditiously to safe ground. On the way back he realizes that being pulled by the strong current has caused him to lose his way. Then the "fissure opens," and he realizes that he may go mad. He decides that "imagination" leads to madness. In this context, "madness" might refer to war in general, to Higginson's present situation, or to his situation as commander of a regiment of ex-slaves. Has he imagined the war as holy cause?

Has he imagined himself as a John Brown-like martyr? Has he imagined that he can swim to the Rebel side and return safely? Has he imagined that he can elevate the ex-slaves by making soldiers of them? Has he imagined he can bridge any "dumb space"? As he reaches safety and steps out of the water in his nakedness (innocence? rebirth?), he comes face to face with the sentinel. The "black statue" who appeared so "dream-like" when Higginson departed has become the "unconscionable fellow" stupidly presenting arms. This episode, beginning as a dream-like product of Higginson's desire, ends as a nightmare. Higginson's attempts to conclude it humorously fail.

A few months later, in July of 1863 during a Confederate attack, Higginson received a blow to the stomach that left him badly bruised. At that point, his interest in the war began to wane until, less than a year later, he resigned, attributing his resignation to "disability resulting from wound." Before he left, he wrote in his journal that "my mind naturally turns to home associations & all other beauty has a vague and alien look; I cannot bring it near to me." He had written his wife that he would support them "from literature" (Edelstein 294–95). Higginson returned to New England and became a famous writer.

In December of 1862, Oliver Wendell Holmes published in the *Atlantic* an essay entitled "My Hunt After the Captain," the story of his journey to find his son Oliver Wendell Holmes, Jr., who had been wounded at Antietam. Before he begins his narration, Holmes insists that readers "must let me tell my story in my own way, speaking of many little matters that interested or amused me." He explains that "anxiety and weariness," rather than preventing him from taking interest in matters around him, had the opposite effect, and "acted like a diffused stimulus upon the attention. When all the faculties are wide-awake in pursuit of a single object, or fixed in the spasm of an absorbing emotion, they are oftentimes clairvoyant in a marvelous degree in respect to many collateral things" (738–39). Thus before the story even begins, Holmes has constructed an incongruous rhetorical situation. The reader wonders whether he will tell the story as doctor, as father, or as traveler and what these other "little matters" are that interest and amuse.

As Holmes sets out by railway to find his son, the journey from Boston to rural Maryland is not so direct as he might have imagined. His "hunt" twists, turns, interrupts itself and is interrupted by outside forces. As the narrator meets with surprises, disappointments, and diversions, the discourse vacillates, leaps, and digresses, and the writer's voice shifts as it moves among various roles—spectator, reporter, interpreter, man of letters, Unionist, friend, doctor, father. Holmes's article, then, is a pastiche made up of a travel story, a father's search for his wounded son, narratives of other men and women on similar "hunts," two eulogies, conversations with Rebel soldiers held as prisoners, comparisons between Boston and other cities, visits to battlefields and hospitals, visits to modern constructions such as New York's Central Park and Philadelphia's water works, descriptions of the wounded and his reactions to them, characterizations of people he meets, and even a digression on plagiarism.

The article begins and ends with the train and with what Holmes calls "locomotive intoxication," a condition where his thoughts get "shaken up by the vibrations into all sorts of new and pleasing patterns . . . fresh ideas coming up to the surface . . . without volition, the mechanical impulse alone keeping the thoughts in motion." Looking out the window, Holmes perceives the rapid movements of near objects and the slow or backward motion of the distant one and concludes that the "whole landscape becomes a mighty wheel revolving about an imaginary axis somewhere in the middle-distance" (739).

While Holmes fantasizes about the generative power of locomotion, however, he notices canal boats, drawn along by mules, and longs with a "mighty passion" to become a canal-boat captain, "to glide back and forward upon a sea never roughened by storms, to float where I could not sink, to navigate where there is no shipwreck, to lie languidly on the deck and govern the huge craft by a word or the movement of a finger" (740). The next day out of Philadelphia, he sees a sentry guarding a railroad bridge and is reminded that he is near "perilous borders . . . where the extremes of our so-called civilization meet in conflict" (741).

As Holmes's observations and reveries indicate, his "perilous borders" are multiple, the obvious ones being between North and South, peace and war, order and chaos, and life and death. But Holmes also feels himself on the edge of something more nebulous—the division between the rapidly moving world of machine technology and the stable, safe world of canals and boats. While the train drives him, a willing passenger, into a delightful place where thoughts are shaken and landscapes become wheels, he yearns for another, more familiar place in the past that he can govern "by a word or a movement of a finger." The longing for a return to patriarchal control is made even more poignant when for days he is unable to locate his son.

After searching makeshift hospitals near battlefields, Holmes returns to Harrisburg, Pennsylvania, only to discover that "the Captain" is still in Maryland but will take the train to Harrisburg the next day. Waiting for his son's train, Holmes now perceives railway transportation as dangerous, with too much potential for collision and a general "want of care for the safety of the people standing around" the stations (759). Finally the expected train arrives, and, walking through the cars, Holmes finds "my Captain."

Returning with his son through Philadelphia, Holmes discovers that the Upper Ferry Bridge across the Schuylkill River has been replaced with a less impressive suspension bridge. In New York, father and son stay in a hotel where instead of climbing stairs they ride to their room on a "vertical railway," a "giant corkscrew" that pulls a "mammoth cork" with carpeting and cushioned seats. While the son rests, the father visits the newly created Central Park where the "roads were fine, the sheets of water beautiful, the bridges handsome, the swans elegant . . . and the grass green" but "its artificial reservoirs" did not compare favorably with the "broad natural sheet of Jamaica Pond" in Boston (763). The train passes town after town on the way home until at last "one fair bosom of the three-hilled city, with its dome-crowned summit, reveals itself, as when many-breasted Ephesian Artemis appeared with half-open *chlamys* before her worshippers" (764). Finally the wounded hero is safe at home in his room where the "shelves [are] thick-set with the names of poets and philosophers and sacred teachers, in whose pages our boys learn that life is noble only when it is held cheap by the side of honor and of duty." Holmes ends with reference to the biblical story of the prodigal son: "this our son and brother was dead and is alive again, and was lost and is found" (764).

Holmes has returned with his son to the safety of Boston and home, an environment populated by philosophers, poets, sacred teachers, and books. In the Boston Holmes has created, safety manifests itself through reference to the past, a past where fatherly poets and philosophers were so powerful that at their approach virgin goddesses revealed themselves without even being asked and where patriarchal authority exerts itself merely "with a word or the movement of a finger."

Nevertheless, the safe world Holmes has created for himself and his son is illusive. As Holmes seems to realize as he longs for the simplicity of canal boats, the authority of the New England intelligentsia has been shattered by the war. Where before the war America struck a precarious balance between modern industrial technology and traditional authority, the outcome of the war ensured a future United States governed not by benevolent patriarchs and their universal principles but by industrial capitalists and their machines. As Holmes observed, it was becoming a world of trains, bridges, elevators, and landscaped parks, whose attempts to impose rational and civilized order destroyed what he considered natural. Substituted in nature's place eventually would be telegraph and telephone lines, water, gas, and sewer lines, houses, towns, factories, streets, roads, highways and finally televisions, airplanes, and computers.

When the nation went to war against itself, "power of character" lost its effectiveness as rhetorical ethos. As rhetoric gave way to violence, "power of character" was replaced by power of force. After the war, these four New England writers retreated from violence and uncertainty by continuing to lecture and write "literature" as if nothing had changed. But as Holmes observed about the train, the world was a place where things, people, and principles collided. The Enlightenment/Unitarian dream of moral and intellectual progress that relied upon patriarchal authority became a nightmare like the nightmarish crisis of faith Higginson experienced in the water off Port Royal. And the Fathers' will, no matter how disinterested and benevolent, could not restore the past. The genteel rhetoric of the Scots, the Unitarians, and the writers of the New England Renaissance became increasingly irrelevant and quaint, eventually retreating behind the walls of the academy, as other voices, some of them passionate, refused to remain silent.

Works Cited

Allen, Gay Wilson. *Waldo Emerson: A Biography.* New York: Viking, 1981.

Anderson, Benedict. *Imagined Communities.* Rev. ed. New York: Verso, 1991.

Aristotle. *Rhetoric.* Trans. W. Rhys Roberts. New York: Random, 1954.

Arnold, Matthew. *Culture and Anarchy.* 1932. Ed. J. Dover Wilson. New York: Cambridge UP, 1960.

Bakhtin, M. M. *The Dialogic Imagination.* Trans. Caryl Emerson and Michael Holquist. Ed. Michael Holquist. Austin: U of Texas P, 1981.

Barthes, Roland. *Mythologies.* New York: Noonday, 1972.

Bartlett, Irving H. *Wendell Phillips, Brahmin Radical.* Boston: Beacon P, 1961.

Bercovitch, Sacvan. *The Rites of Assent.* New York: Routledge, 1993.

Berlin, James A. "Poststructuralism, Semiotics, and Social-Epistemic Rhetoric." In *Defining the New Rhetorics,* ed. Theresa Enos and Stuart C. Brown. Newbury Park: Sage, 1993.

———. "Revisionary Histories of Rhetoric." In *Writing Histories of Rhetoric,* ed. Victor J. Vitanza. Carbondale: Southern Illinois UP, 1994.

———. *Writing Instruction in Nineteenth-Century American Colleges.* Carbondale: Southern Illinois UP, 1984.

Blair, Hugh. *Lectures on Rhetoric and Belles Lettres.* Philadelphia: Hayes & Zell, 1858.

Bourdieu, Pierre. *Distinction.* Cambridge: Harvard UP, 1984.

———. *Language and Symbolic Power.* Ed. John B. Thompson. Cambridge: Harvard UP, 1991.

Braverman, Harry. *Labor and Monopoly Capital.* New York: Monthly Review P, 1974.

Brooks, Van Wyck. *The Life of Emerson.* New York: Literary Guild, 1932.

Buell, Lawrence. *New England Literary Culture.* Cambridge: Cambridge UP, 1986.

Bushman, Richard L. *The Refinement of America.* New York: Vintage, 1992.

Certeau, Michel de. *The Practice of Everyday Life.* Berkeley: U of California P, 1984.

Channing, Edward Tyrell. *Lectures Read to the Seniors in Harvard College.* Ed. Dorothy I. Anderson and Waldo W. Braden. Carbondale: Southern Illinois UP, 1968.

———. "Life of William Ellery." In *The Library of American Biography,* vol. 6, ed. Jared Sparks. Boston: Hilliard, Gray, 1839.

Channing, William Ellery. *Discourses on War.* Boston: Ginn, 1903.

———. "On the Elevation of the Laboring Classes." In *Essays: English and American,* ed. Charles W. Eliot. The Harvard Classics. New York: P. F. Collier, 1910.

———. *Self-Culture.* Boston: James Munroe, 1845.

———. *Slavery and Emancipation.* 1836. New York: Negro Universities P, 1968.

Channing, William Henry. *Memoir of William Ellery Channing.* Vol. 1. Boston: Wm. Crosby & H. P. Nichols, 1848. 3 vols.

Cicero. *De Inventione.* Cambridge, Harvard UP, 1949.

Clark, Gregory, and S. Michael Halloran, eds. *Oratorical Culture in Nineteenth-Century America.* Carbondale: Southern Illinois UP, 1993.

Connors, Robert J. "Women's Reclamation of Rhetoric in Nineteenth-Century America." In *Feminine Principles and Women's Experience in American Composition and Rhetoric,* ed. Louise Wetherbee Phelps and Janet Emig. Pittsburgh: U of Pittsburgh P, 1995.

Cook, Roy J., ed. *One Hundred and One Famous Poems.* Chicago: Reilly & Lee, 1958.

Dana, Richard Henry, Jr. Biographical Notice. In *Lectures Read to the Seniors in Harvard College,* by Edward T. Channing. Ed. Dorothy I. Anderson and Waldo W. Braden. Carbondale: Southern Illinois UP, 1968.

Deleuze, Gilles, and Felix Guattari. *Anti-Oedipus.* Trans. Robert Hurley, Mark Seem, and Helen R. Lane. Minneapolis: U of Minnesota P, 1983.

Donald, David. *Charles Sumner and the Coming of the Civil War.* New York: Alfred A. Knopf, 1960.

Duberman, Martin. *James Russell Lowell.* Boston: Houghton Mifflin, 1966.

Du Bois, W. E. B. *The Souls of Black Folk.* New York: Vintage, 1990.

Edelstein, Leon. *Strange Enthusiasm.* New Haven: Yale UP, 1968.

Edgell, David P. *William Ellery Channing: An Intellectual Portrait.* Boston: Beacon P, 1955.

Emerson, Ralph Waldo. "American Civilization." *Atlantic Monthly,* April 1862: 502–11.

———. *Complete Works.* Vols. 7 and 12. Cambridge: Riverside, 1883. 12 vols.

———. *Emerson's Anti-Slavery Writings.* Ed. Len Gougeon and Joel Myerson. New Haven: Yale UP, 1995.

———. *Essays: First and Second Series.* New York: Vintage, 1990.

———. *Selected Prose and Poetry.* Ed. Reginald L. Cook. New York: Holt, 1950.

———. *Two Unpublished Essays.* Ed. Edward Everett Hale. Boston: Lamson-Wolffe, 1895.

———. *The Works of Ralph Waldo Emerson.* Vols. 1 and 2. New York: Tudor, 1930. 4 vols.

Everett, Edward. *Orations and Speeches on Various Occasions.* Vol. 1. Boston: Little Brown, 1850–1868. 4 vols.

Floan, Howard R. *The South in Northern Eyes 1831–1861.* Austin: U of Texas P, 1958.

Foner, Eric. *Politics and Ideology in the Age of the Civil War.* New York: Oxford UP, 1980.

Foner, Eric, and John A. Garraty, eds. *The Reader's Companion to American History.* Boston: Houghton Mifflin, 1991.

Foucault, Michel. *The Order of Things.* New York: Vintage, 1973.

Fredrickson, George M. *The Black Image in the White Mind.* New York: Harper & Row, 1972.

———. *The Inner Civil War.* Urbana: U of Illinois P, 1993.

Gougeon, Len. *Virtue's Hero.* Athens: U of Georgia P, 1990.

Green, Martin. *The Problem of Boston.* New York: W. W. Norton, 1967.

Hall, Peter Dobkin. *The Organization of American Culture, 1700–1900.* New York: New York UP, 1982.

Heymann, C. David. *American Aristocracy.* New York: Dodd Mead, 1980.

Higginson, Thomas Wentworth. *Army Life in a Black Regiment.* East Lansing: Michigan State UP, 1960.

———. *Book and Heart.* New York: Harper, 1897.

———. *Cheerful Yesterdays.* New York: Houghton Mifflin, 1898.

———. *Contemporaries.* Upper Saddle River, N.J.: Literature House, 1970.

———. "Denmark Vesey." *Atlantic Monthly,* June 1861: 728–44.

———. *Hints on Writing and Speech-Making.* Boston: Lee & Shepard, 1887.

———. "Literature as an Art." *Atlantic Monthly,* Dec. 1867: 745–54.

———. "Nat Turner's Insurrection." *Atlantic Monthly,* Aug. 1861: 173–87.

Holmes, Oliver Wendell. *The Autocrat of the Breakfast Table.* Boston: Houghton Mifflin, 1890.

———. *Elsie Venner.* Cambridge: Riverside P, 1892.

———. "My Hunt After the Captain." *Atlantic Monthly,* Dec. 1862: 736–64.

———. *Pages From an Old Volume of Life.* Cambridge: Riverside P, 1893.

———. *Ralph Waldo Emerson.* Boston: Houghton, 1885.

Howe, Daniel Walker. *The Unitarian Conscience.* Cambridge: Harvard UP, 1970.

Howe, M. A. DeWolfe. *Boston.* New York: Macmillan, 1903.

Hoyt, Edwin P. *The Improper Bostonian.* New York: William Morrow, 1979.

Hutcheson, Francis. *An Inquiry into the Original of Our Ideas of Beauty and Virtue.* 1726. New York: Garland, 1971.

———. *A Short Introduction to Moral Philosophy.* 1747. Ann Arbor: University Microfilms, 1969.

Kasson, John F. *Civilizing the Machine.* New York: Penguin, 1988.

———. *Rudeness and Civility.* New York: Hill & Wang, 1990.

Kennedy, George A. *Classical Rhetoric and Its Christian and Secular Tradition from Ancient to Modern Times.* Chapel Hill: U of North Carolina P, 1980.

Kitzhaber, Albert R. *Rhetoric in American Colleges, 1850–1900.* Dallas: Southern Methodist UP, 1990.

Lears, T. J. Jackson. "The Concept of Cultural Hegemony: Problems and Possibilities." *American Historical Review* 90 (June 1985): 567–593.

Leverenz, David. *Manhood and the American Renaissance.* Ithaca: Cornell UP, 1989.

Levine, Lawrence W. *Highbrow/Lowbrow.* Cambridge: Harvard UP, 1988.

Lewis, R. W. B. *The American Adam.* Chicago: U of Chicago P, 1955.

Lovejoy, Arthur O. *The Great Chain of Being.* 1936. Cambridge: Harvard UP, 1982.

Lowell, James Russell. *The Anti-Slavery Papers of James Russell Lowell.* Vol. 1 New York: Negro Universities P, 1969. 2 vols.

———. *The Biglow Papers.* 2d Series. Boston: Ticknor & Fields, 1867.

———. *Democracy and Other Addresses.* Boston: Houghton Mifflin, 1887.

———. *Lowell's Prose Works.* Vol. 3. Boston: Houghton Mifflin, 1892. 10 vols.

———. *My Study Windows.* Boston: Houghton Mifflin, 1913.

———. "Nationality in Literature." *North American Review,* July 1849: 196–215.

———. *The Poetical Works of James Russell Lowell.* Boston: Houghton Mifflin, 1978.

———. *Political Essays.* Cambridge: Riverside, 1904.

May, Henry F. *The Enlightenment in America.* New York: Oxford UP, 1976.

McFague, Sallie. *Metaphorical Theology.* Philadelphia: Fortress P, 1982.

Miller, Perry, ed. *The American Transcendentalists.* Baltimore: Johns Hopkins UP, 1957.

Morison, Samuel Eliot. *Three Centuries of Harvard, 1636–1936.* Cambridge: Belknap P, 1964.

Newfield, Christopher. *The Emerson Effect.* Chicago: U of Chicago P, 1996.

Niven, John. *The Coming of the Civil War 1837–1861.* Arlington Heights: Harlan Davidson, 1990.

Pease, Donald E. "Author." In *Critical Terms for Literary Study,* ed. Frank Lentricchia and Thomas McLaughlin. Chicago: U of Chicago P, 1990.

Perelman, Ch., and L. Olbrechts-Tyteca. *The New Rhetoric.* Trans. John Wilkinson and Purcell Weaver. Notre Dame: U of Notre Dame P, 1971.

Porte, Joel. *Representative Man: Ralph Waldo Emerson in His Time.* New York: Oxford UP, 1979.

Pratt, Mary Louise. *Imperial Eyes: Travel Writing and Transculturation.* New York: Routledge, 1992.

Quintilian. *On the Early Education of the Citizen-Orator.* Indianapolis: Bobbs-Merrill, 1965.

Ravitch, Diane, ed. *The American Reader.* New York: HarperCollins, 1990.

Reid, Thomas. *Philosophical Works.* 2 vols. 1895. Ed. Sir William Hamilton. Hildeshein: Olms, 1967.

Robinson, David, ed. *William Ellery Channing: Selected Writings:* New York: Paulist P, 1985.

Said, Edward. *Culture and Imperialism.* New York: Vintage, 1994.

Sedgwick, Ellery. *A History of the Atlantic Monthly 1857–1909.* Amherst: U of Massachusetts P, 1994.

Sekora, John. "Mr. Editor, If You Please." *Callaloo* 17, no. 2 (1994): 608–26.

Sellers, Charles. *The Market Revolution.* New York: Oxford UP, 1991.

Sennett, Richard. *Authority.* New York: Vintage, 1981.

Simpson, Lewis. "The Intercommunity of the Learned." *New England Quarterly* 28 (1950): 490–503.

Sloan, Douglas. *The Scottish Enlightenment and the American College Ideal.* New York: Teachers College P, 1971.

Smith, Adam. *The Theory of Moral Sentiments.* London: Bahn, 1853.

Solomon, Barbara Miller. *Ancestors and Immigrants.* 1956. Boston: Northeastern UP, 1989.

Spencer, Benjamin. *The Quest for Nationality.* Syracuse: Syracuse UP, 1957.

Stanton, William. *The Leopard's Spots.* Chicago: U of Chicago P, 1960.

Story, Ronald. *The Forging of an Aristocracy.* Middletown: Wesleyan UP, 1980.

Sumner, Charles. *The Crime Against Kansas.* New York: Arno P, 1969.

Takaki, Ronald. *Iron Cages.* New York: Alfred A. Knopf, 1979.

Thompson, John B. Editor's Introduction. In *Language and Symbolic Power,* by Pierre Bourdieu. Cambridge: Harvard UP, 1991.

Thornton, Tamara Plakins. *Cultivating Gentlemen.* New Haven: Yale UP, 1989.

Tuttleton, James W. *Thomas Wentworth Higginson.* Boston: Twayne, 1978.

Varg, Paul A. *Edward Everett.* Selinsgrove: Susquehanna UP, 1992.

Webster, Daniel. *The Works of Daniel Webster.* Vol. 2. Boston: Little, Brown, 1854. 6 vols.

Wendell, Barrett. *Literary History of America.* 3rd ed. New York: Charles Scribner's Sons, 1901.

Williams, Raymond. *The Long Revolution.* New York: Columbia UP, 1961.

Wilson, Douglas L., ed. *The Genteel Tradition: Nine Essays by George Santayana.* Cambridge: Harvard UP, 1967.

Wilson, Edmund. *Patriotic Gore.* New York: W. W. Norton, 1962.

Wood, Gordon S. *The Creation of the American Republic, 1776–1787.* New York: W. W. Norton, 1969.

Wortham, Thomas. "Did Emerson Blackball Frederick Douglass From Membership in the Town and Country Club?" *The New England Quarterly* June 1992: 295–98.

Index